DON'T WAIT TOO LONG

Paul Stutzman

All scripture quoted from the Holy Bible, New International Version®, NIV ®. Copyright© 1973, 1978, 1984, 2011 by Biblica, Inc.™ Used by permission of Zondervan. All rights reserved worldwide.

Scripture quotations marked NLT are taken from the Holy Bible, New Living Translation, copyright © 1996, 2004, 2015 by Tyndale House Foundation. Used by permission of Tyndale House Publishers, Inc., Carol Stream, Illinois 60188. All rights reserved.

Scripture quotes marked (AP) are the author's paraphrase.

Copyright © 2019, 2022 Wandering Home Books
All rights reserved. No part of this publication may be reproduced, stored in a retrieval system or transmitted, in any form, or by any means, electronic, mechanical, photocopying, recording, or otherwise, without the prior permission of the publisher.

ISBN 13: 978-0-9998874-3-1

Part 1 DON'T WAIT TOO LONG

Don't Wait Too Long 3

Spiritual Romance 8

Guard Your Heart 11

Growing Up Loved 14

Golden Days of Love 18

Limit, One per Pedestal 20

From the Pedestal to the Stone 22

Part 2 THE IN-BETWEEN

The In-Between 27

The Valley of Decision 30

Swamp Creatures 32

"Trust Me" 35

So Lonely, I Cried 37

The Alabaster Heart 41

Come and See 46

Jesus, the Forsaken Scapegoat 49

Self-Judgment 52

Jesus, the Curtain 55

The Yoke's on You 58

"Lord, Save Me!" 60

"Lord, Save Me, Too!" 64

Saved and Rescued 68

Storms 73

Sandcastles 75

Sowing and Reaping... 78

Deception 81

Dilemma 88

The Cost of Unforgiveness 91

5,000 Steps in the Wilderness 94

Be Honorable 96

Rejection... 99

Rejection Survival Guide 103

Heart Condition 106

Double-Minded Hearts.. 109

Plowed Heart.. 112

The Stained-Glass Heart 114

You Are Loved 116

"Come and Dine"... 118

Monarchs.. 122

Introspection 125

Darkening Chrysalis... 128

Butterfly.. 134

Part 3 BECOMING ENOCH

Expiration Dates... 139

Enoch 142

Diverging Pathways 147

God's Thoughts 151

Mystery 153

The Interpreter	158
Knowing the Holy Spirit	162
The Counselor's Residence	165
Prayer Guide	168
Lonely Places to Pray	170
God Speaking	172
Signs from God	174
Don't Wait	177
Making Hard Choices	179
Answered Prayer	182
Signpost #91	186
Writing Your Book?	189
Plowing Straight	193
Distractions	196
From Strength to Strength	199
The Big Picture	202
Parable of the Lost Key	206
Poured Out	210
The Birthday Story	216
Active Wisdom	219
Words Have Meaning	222
Delightful, Delicious, Protective Words	225
Sheep and Goats	227
The Least of These	231
Who Is Your Neighbor?	237

Weary Pilgrim 242

The Eternal Gift 244

Godly Investments 247

Return to Blueberry Patch 250

The Redemption of Jill 255

Mystery in the Mist 258

Heroes 261

Lights in the Valley 264

And Then What? 267

God of Truth 270

The Real Life 273

Joint Heirs with Jesus 276

Becoming my Father 279

Lighten Up 282

Let Us Faith the Truth 284

The First Supper 288

Going Even Deeper 293

Author's Note 299

Part 1

DON'T WAIT TOO LONG

Don't Wait Too Long

I was at peace. All was right with the world.
And then life got even better.
Until it went to worse, and then plunged to worst.
But worst eventually turned, and now I'm headed toward best.
Stay with me, and you'll hear the story.

I had finally made the honorable decision. For several years, I'd been selfish and less than honorable. But now I'd done the right thing, and I was at peace. The decision I made also opened the door to a chain of events that has led to you holding this book right now.

For some reason, it seems I've always had to learn life lessons the hard way. Perhaps my stumbling can save you weeks or even years of pain. Whether you're a man or a woman, feel free to learn from my mistakes. My story might have its own unique personal details, but the principles God has established are universal and applicable to all of life.

I had been selfish, and that trait will not nurture a healthy relationship. However, I know I'm not alone. Selfishness is the cause of so many problems in life, and often, we don't even recognize that trait in ourselves.

Following the death of my wife, Mary, I was a bit unmoored. It's a common state for many men who have lost a spouse after a lengthy marriage. We have so much pain and loneliness to deal with that we grasp at any relief, whether temporary or permanent. I was no exception. I reached out to a woman who had been in a difficult marriage but was then praying diligently for a godly husband.

She believed I qualified as that. I did not.

However, I kept seeing her for a season. Then I'd initiate short periods of separation. Acute loneliness resulted, and I'd begin another season of seeing her.

In 2016, decision time came. In the fall, I spent several weeks hiking in Israel. During my time there, I contemplated what it meant to follow Jesus. I wanted a clearer vision for my life. I was also contemplating that ongoing relationship back home. When I left the U.S., my friend had given the directive to have my answer when I returned home. Should I stay in the relationship, or end it?

I determined it was best to be apart. I did not realize how that decision crushed her dream and her spirit. I thought she was an emotionally strong person who could accept my choice and move on with her life, but she was headed for a year of heartbreak and pain. She finally gave her all to God and became a whole, godly woman. She now leads a ministry for hurting women.

Me? I spent the next two months at home, waiting on God. I rarely left the house. In a two-month timeframe, I had only one social event. But for the first time in years, I felt at peace with God and myself.

It had been ten years, though, since my wife died, and although my life had been filled with adventures, books to write, and speaking engagements, I was tired of doing life alone. I wanted to share it intimately with someone. My prayer then was that if it were possible, I wanted to feel love again. I wanted a love like we experience when we first feel that love for a special person.

God, is that even possible at my age?

Yes! It's possible.

One evening in late January of 2017, an email arrived from a lady whose husband had passed away. Although his recent health had not allowed strenuous activity, he had enjoyed hiking in his younger days. This man had purchased my book *Hiking Through* and read the story of a man who made a difficult choice, a choice to not wait too long to enjoy the blessings of life. The man was financially able to retire early, and that became his plan. He sent a note to his best friend, who also enjoyed the outdoors and hiking, and recommended that he, too, read *Hiking Through*.

Then this man suddenly became deathly ill. The diagnosis was cancer, and within two weeks, the man died. During those final two weeks of his shortened life, he dreamed of writing a book encouraging people not to wait too long to retire and follow their dreams. But he never had the chance to pen his thoughts.

Following his passing, his friend told the widow that *Hiking Through* was somewhere in her husband's library. It was about hiking the Appalachian Trail to find peace after the loss of a spouse.

6 DON'T WAIT **TOO LONG**

The grieving wife searched through her husband's books and discovered *Hiking Through.* She had just begun to read it when she emailed me and relayed her husband's desire to write a book about "not waiting too long." She inquired about the book-writing process, thinking that perhaps she herself should author the book.

I've received several thousand emails and letters in response to *Hiking Through.* I can't reply to all of them. However, if someone asks a question, I do reply. This question about writing a book is one I've often been asked. I gave this lady the same response I give others: Whatever you write, convey a message with significance. Your goal in writing is to have the reader close the book the final time and say, "I learned something that will make me a better person."

The message of "Don't wait too long" is also one I've delivered for years. This is one of those lessons that I've learned through pain. That's why I encourage people to enjoy the journey now. Don't wait for someday.

Mary and I worked hard all of our married life. At times, too hard. It's what so many couples do. The plan is to work hard, get out of debt, and someday retire and then do things we "want" to do. Mary and I dreamed of retiring in our late fifties and giving time to volunteer work. But for many of us, while we're still looking ahead for "someday" to arrive, house payments, raising kids, college debt, career building, and countless other issues distract us from the real joy of everyday living.

Mary and I waited too long.

One day in May, I rushed into Mary's hospital room in great excitement. I showed her the bank coupon—the last one! "Honey, it's our last house payment. We are completely out of debt! Finally!"

She looked at me sadly and quietly said, "Yes, that's great."
But it wasn't. Four months later, my wife passed away.

We had too often missed the joy of the journey by postponing daily joys and looking only toward future possibilities.

How about you? Are you waiting for that elusive someday to really enjoy life?

Don't wait too long.

2

Spiritual Romance

In my reply to this widow's email and inquiry about book writing, I took the liberty of asking if she had joined a grief support group. She sent a reply and then also asked how my three children worked through the grieving process. She had two daughters who loved their dad dearly and were hurting so much.

Again, I answered, and a pattern developed. Each email we sent ended with a question requiring a reply. After every few chapters she read in *Hiking Through,* she emailed me her thoughts on those chapters and how they were helping her deal with her grief.

When she discovered I had written other books, she soon purchased those, too. The book reports kept coming. A bond between us was slowly forming, and I felt comfortable enough to ask in one email if she would be willing to speak with me on a phone call. She was. We did.

For me, a five-minute phone call is usually four minutes too long. Our first phone conversation went on for fifty minutes. Our discussion flowed easily, and soon we were speaking every day.

"Would you like to meet?" I asked. She lived in another state.

"Let me pray about it, and I'll let you know."

The following day, she told me she had prayed about our meeting and felt at peace with it. I was in Florida on a short vacation when she gave me her answer. In a few days, I would be heading toward home in Ohio and could easily stop for a brief visit. We chose a meeting place.

The anticipation of the unknown caused some anxiety, to be sure. This was uncharted territory for both of us. Since we had exchanged many phone calls, emails, and texts, we believed we understood each other's hearts. But what about the rest of us? Our bodies, to be specific. Would I be too short? Would she be too tall? Men are visual creatures, and I'm no exception. I enjoy beauty. Whether it's watching a sunset, or walking through a flower garden, or a mountain top scene, I'm entranced by beauty. God created women beautiful. That's His intention. He created us men to be attracted to beauty, and I am. What did she look like? What would I look like to her eyes?

We both believed our meeting would probably be a short one. Just long enough to convince us there was nothing to see here.

However, there was something to see. We met, and she was beautiful and gracious; and I was apparently acceptable in her eyes, too.

We talked. "I'm glad I'm not too tall," she remarked.

"I'm glad I'm not too short," I replied.

We shared a meal together. I prayed with her, the first of many prayers together. She had even remembered that my birthday was coming up in a few days and had brought a small cake and a gift. I was convinced I had just met the kindest person in my life.

There was not only something to see, there was much to *feel*. We both felt it; we both knew something special was taking place. We both were convinced the way we met was a miracle. God had brought us together by her husband's chance purchase of my book.

My father wrote poetry. Poems flowed easily from his mind. I can write poems myself, but only when deeply in love or deeply suffering. That evening, words of poetry danced through my mind. Conversation flowed freely. I hadn't been this happy in years. God had answered my prayers for love.

During our evening together, we met a woman in tears. She was suffering deeply, having lost two significant people in her life. Her father had recently passed away, and her boyfriend had just broken up with her. We wrapped our arms around this lady and took turns praying for her, taking her pain upon us and lifting her up to God. This kind of encounter would happen frequently during the first year of our relationship.

Beauty, kindness, generosity, and godliness. The Proverbs 31 woman had just been gifted to me by a loving God. Of that I was convinced.

Driving home, I called my new friend and coined a term to describe what we had just experienced.

"That was spiritual romance," I said.

We agreed to meet again.

3

Guard Your Heart

We met again a few weeks later and again, a few weeks after that. An amazing thing began to happen. Folks would approach us and exclaim, "You two are in love! We can see it on your faces." And undoubtedly, we were; and yes, it showed.

The world changes when two people are in love. The sky is bluer, the aroma of flowers is sweeter, and the joy in one's heart has never been greater. That may all sound like a cliché, but it's true!

In Proverbs 4, the writer talks about wisdom. He is speaking as a father to a son.

"Pay attention to me and you will gain understanding. Get wisdom, get understanding. Don't forsake wisdom. She will protect you. She will watch over you. Esteem her, embrace her, and she will honor you." (Wisdom is personified here as a lady.)

The writer of Proverbs continues with many instructions for life and living, given to enhance life and bring health to a man's whole body.

12 DON'T WAIT **TOO LONG**

There's a caveat. An "above all else" instruction. Something even more important than any of the other instructions. Verse 23 of Proverbs 4 counsels, "Above all else, guard your heart, for it is the wellspring of life."

We both gave the guards to our hearts permission to take a siesta.

Guard, guard, listen up. Thanks for keeping us away from others so we two could meet. But take a break for a while. We've got things covered.

We started making plans for our future. Yes, we had some differences in our beliefs; however, we were both Christians, so that could surely all be worked out. Yes, there was a considerable distance between our two homes, but that was a small obstacle that love could surely work out. Love had already built a bridge between our hearts, so love could certainly work out the logistics of distance. Many love songs I'd listened to in the past promised that.

We even became Jesus to folks we met. It was so easy to do. We were in love!

Instead of walking in the opposite direction when we were approached by homeless and downtrodden folks, we now embraced them. One day as we slowly swayed back and forth on a park swing, a young homeless couple approached us. It was a beautiful spring day in a waterfront park. Love was in the air and all around us.

"Could you help us out?" asked the young couple. "We have no money for food."

He was someone's son; she was someone's daughter. That could have been my son or daughter. They were two children loved by God. Bad choices had put them in a bad situation. However, I admit, I was a bit reluctant to give them anything, thinking they might just be looking for money to buy drugs.

My friend looked at me and asked, "Should I help them?"
There was such a look of kindness in her eyes that I immediately said, "Sure, if your heart is telling you to."
"It is," she said. She gave them money.
They didn't leave. The young girl kept staring at my friend with longing eyes. I looked through those eyes and read her soul. That's not possible with everyone; some folks are so hardened with sin and their eyes are so cold they're impossible to read. This girl's eyes still held a longing for hope. She was looking at the kind lady beside me and seeing what she herself could become with better choices. She glimpsed kindness that day. She had been judged harshly by so many, yet now she had met the kindest person ever.
Since they didn't take the money and run, we offered to pray for them. The young man, tattooed and pierced, gave me a confused look and asked, "How's that going to happen?"
"Here's how."
We stood and put our arms around that homeless couple and took turns praying for their safety and for their future. That young couple met Jesus that day in the form of two people deeply in love. In love with Jesus and each other.
The two guards to our hearts had returned from another siesta and lounged nearby, in case they were needed. They weren't.
Guards, take a vacation. Go to some island somewhere. Go on a cruise. We won't be needing your services anymore.

4

Growing Up Loved

My first year with my new friend was wonderful. We talked, laughed, and became Jesus to many folks we met. She met my children and my sisters. Everyone loved her immediately. Her family was a bit more cautious in welcoming this man arriving from Amish Country. However, I was beginning to fall in love with her entire family.

I did what I had been unable or unwilling to do with my previous girlfriend. I gave her my heart with no hesitation or reservation.

My mom and dad were married 68 years. I rarely, if ever, witnessed an argument between them or heard Dad directing his raised voice toward Mom.

My father passed away several years ago. Both he and Mom were in a convalescent center at the time. It was intended to be a brief stay for both. Mom was recovering from surgery, and Dad was being cared for in the same facility just for the duration of Mom's stay.

I visited Dad on a Saturday in May. As I was leaving, I told him I was going to stop over in Mom's room and visit with her a while.

"Oh, I love her so much!" he said.

Imagine that. Almost seventy years of marriage, and still so deeply in love. Those were the last words I would ever hear from my dad. He passed away that night.

The next morning, I headed to Mom's room with trepidation. How would she react? I knelt by her bed, and with tears streaming down my face told her that Dad had passed away during the night.

Imagine my surprise when she raised her hands heavenward and exclaimed, "Oh, that's so good!"

Now, I'm sure there are horrible marriages when a spouse might say that, but why, in such a godly marriage, would a bereaved spouse utter such a thing?

Mom knew something most others did not. She was dying, too. The surgery had gone satisfactorily, but recovery had been difficult. She was only staying alive because she knew Dad needed her.

Several days before her surgery, she had told me she was dying. I refused to believe it at the time, but at her bidding I followed her to a room where she showed me the arrangements she had made for her funeral. She had chosen songs and Scripture readings for the service.

Now, with Dad already in Heaven, she knew her time had come as well. One week later—on Mother's Day—she passed away and joined Dad.

My siblings and I lost both parents in the span of one week. Mom's doctor told us her death was due to complications from surgery and a broken heart.

16 DON'T WAIT **TOO LONG**

Several years prior to their deaths, my parents had suffered a devastating financial blow. Dad was a lifelong saver. We never had much money, but he always had enough to care for his family, tithe, and save a little wherever he could. By the time he retired, he had a considerable savings built up. Mom had also received a modest inheritance from her mom's estate. Sadly, they transferred all their savings into a too-good-to-be-true pyramid scheme run by an investor who promised large returns. They had trusted him, but the pyramid scheme collapsed, and many people lost everything. My mom and dad were among the largest claimants.

After receiving the news, I stopped in at their house that evening. I was leaving on a five-thousand-mile bicycle trip across America the following morning and wanted to offer them condolences on their loss.

Imagine my surprise when I found them sitting on the couch holding hands, singing a song about God's goodness.

Who does that? My parents!

As a child, I would lie in bed and listen to Mom and Dad sing before retiring for the night. I used to think every child went to bed hearing their parents sing. I used to think every child was loved like we children were. I now know that wasn't the case, and I realize how fortunate we were.

That night, I asked Mom if they weren't worried about the money they had lost. "Certainly we are," she said, "but our trust is in God, not our money."

That was my family.

It's said we turn out like our parents unless we make a deliberate effort to change. In my case, there was no need to change. If I were to turn out like Dad, some lady would indeed be blessed with a good man.

Unfortunately, I had a few character flaws that were quite unlike Dad. I became a bit selfish. That does not lend itself to a godly relationship. My father never exhibited even an inkling of selfishness. He didn't pass that character quality on to me. I allowed the devil a bit of control in my life. Everything became about *me*.

When God gifted me this great love again, I became my dad. I loved the way I had seen my parents love. I gave my new friend my heart, my trust, and all my hopes for the future, and in return, she gave me hers.

The guards to our hearts and minds were now in the witness protection program out in some far western state. They weren't needed and were afraid to even approach us.

5

Golden Days of Love

A year of love passed quickly. We even had all our favorite songs on a CD. We sent each other love songs that spoke to us, and she, being a determined lady, learned how to download music. The resulting CD was filled with precious memories of a golden summer in love.

She kept Hallmark solvent during our relationship, with an uncanny ability to pick out a card that precisely conveyed the right message needed at the right moment. She also kept her local post office busy sending out cards and packages, and I loved going to my post office and picking up those cards and packages. A drawer in my bedroom was stuffed full of cards and mementos.

Every night, we had telephone conversations. I can recall only two nights over the next two years that we did not speak.

Thanks to her generosity, I crossed off many things on my bucket list. For example, I had often read about the feeling of quiet freedom experienced by those who sail. One day I remarked that I've always wanted to go sailing.

"I have an uncle in Florida who has a sailboat. He sails to the Keys, to Cuba, to the Bahamas," she said.

Could it be possible to go sailing with her uncle? But of course it was. We went sailing.

As the end of the first year of love approached, I made a mistake my dad would never have made. I waited too long. Had I proposed marriage then, she would have accepted, and we would now be enjoying our happily-ever-after. "Don't Wait Too Long" had initiated our meeting in the first place. How ironic if it was to be the reason this love story ended.

Since our guards were dismissed from duty and no longer available for counsel, I erred grievously. I surrendered the place in my heart that belonged to God; I gave it to Her.

Please listen. This is vital. Don't ever give the space in your heart that belongs to God to any person—not to someone you're in love with, not to your child, not to a friend, not to your leader or mentor. Giving God's place to anyone else is a guarantee of disaster. Guarding God's hallowed place won't keep your heart from being broken, but recovery will be easier if God is at the center of your life, in that place where He alone belongs.

Allowing a person to take control of God's place will work—until it doesn't. And when it doesn't, you will be left with a completely empty heart. Should your guard happen to get lonely and return, it will be guarding an empty tomb. Nothing coming out, nothing going in, except loneliness and despair.

6

Limit, One per Pedestal

I had put my friend up on a pedestal. She certainly didn't ask to be put there. I did it willingly. I looked in admiration at someone who was so kind and so good. If she had flaws, I either missed them or overlooked them.

But of course, we all have flaws. Love often overlooks or avoids dealing with potential pitfalls in a relationship. *Oh, it will work out. Love will find a way.* That's a line I used several times in our relationship. When I said it, I fervently believed it to be true. However, I was too busy enjoying being in love to contemplate how the "it will work out" part might actually work out.

I was treated so kindly by my friend that I started to believe I deserved to be treated that well. I also believed there was room on that pedestal for me.

There wasn't.

But I tried, yes, I did. I climbed to the lofty heights to which I had elevated her, and the view was grand. Unfortunately, I blocked her view and got pushed off.

From that lofty perch, she surveyed the landscape and a man appeared who seemed better suited for her. In an instant, everything I believed about our love came crashing down.

7

From the Pedestal to the Stone

In the months since my fall from the pedestal, I've discovered Matthew 21:44: "He who falls on this stone will be broken to pieces, but he on whom it falls will be crushed."

I'm aware that some Biblical scholars have interpreted this Scripture as a reference to punishment by stoning, but it has spoken to me about being broken. I like to think of this stone as Jesus, and a person coming with a contrite heart can fall on Jesus and be broken open. It is a necessary breaking, an utterly painful breaking, but a breaking that will lead to wholeness.

My plummet from the pedestal was just such a landing. My spirit was crushed. My heart broken. One minute before, I was on top of the world. In an instant, my hopes and dreams were crushed.

What happened?

I believe God intends for most of us to journey through life with a partner, a companion. Our journey is just easier when two people live and love as a godly couple. With the distance between us, we found it difficult to spend as much time together as we would have liked. When I left her house and returned home, I was at peace and contented since I had her love and support. She, however, missed that daily interaction with a loving companion. It caused her to consider other options, and she easily found one. She easily moved on. I didn't. I was blindsided and devastated.

How, God, how could that happen to me? Didn't you bring us together? We both believed that in the beginning. How could it end so badly?

But it had and it did. I was a broken man.

How does one heal from such a devastating blow? There is only one way, and that is to go to the one who will never let you down—Jesus.

This is where the love stories of my past two years meet. Perhaps love stories have no appeal for you and you're already thinking of giving up on this book. Wait! There's an even better love story coming. It's not about my pursuit of romance, but about heights and depths of love, adventure, and *life* that you cannot even imagine.

This love story is so important that it will make all the difference in your journey on this earth.

Part 2
THE IN-BETWEEN

8

The In-Between

If the span of our years was laid out into four equal seasons, we could prepare for the seasonal changes in life. Live eighty years, have four equal seasons of twenty years. There's plenty of time to plan and prepare for whatever changes the next season will bring.

As winter changes into spring or summer into fall, there are some "in-between" days. On some days, winter prods its cold claws into spring, where it certainly does not belong. On other in-between days, a morning chill and frost of fall reach back into summer.

As we live toward our death, we have those in-between days as well. They are not expected or planned for. They are oftentimes unsettling. They are disorienting. We aren't exactly sure where we are or what's ahead of us.

As I write this book, I'm at an in-between. I'm in between pain and joy. The season of joy is ahead, I'm certain, yet the season of pain keeps intruding, pulling me backwards at the same time joy tugs me forward.

28 DON'T WAIT **TOO LONG**

There are those moments when I'm in between the devil and Jesus. The devil says, *You've been rejected. You're worth nothing.* Jesus says, *I've chosen you. You're worth everything.*

Those days we live in the in-between are often very trying times. However, as we reflect back on our seasons, I would guess those are times of growth. At times, it's painful growth. Dragged-kicking-and-screaming growth. Growth forced by having to live between loss and gain.

Life has often been compared to living in valleys and on mountaintops. Even those who've never stood on a mountain understand the metaphor of "mountaintop experiences." We all love those. Mountaintop living is grand. The view to the future is pleasant. We settle into our normal routines. The memory of the last in-between valley has been filed away in a corner of our memory bank. Our minds don't want to acknowledge there could be another valley awaiting.

But invariably, there is another valley on the other side of the mountain. Another season of life approaching. Another in-between time of trials and struggles.

The valleys are what make mountaintop living so rewarding. You'll have to experience pain to understand pleasure. You'll have to endure sadness to fully enjoy happiness. Can you really appreciate the true value of trust if someone has never broken your trust?

The valleys are the wilderness experiences through which we travel, the in-between times that separate our seasons of mountaintop living.

The same valleys that separate us from the mountaintops also connect us to the next mountain. We're going to revisit several Biblical accounts that hold truth for our lives. I'll give you this assignment in advance: Notice how many significant, life-changing things have happened in the lonely-place wilderness. In the account of the temptation of Jesus, for example, notice this important detail: Jesus went into the wilderness because He was led there by the Holy Spirit.

Have I been led here, Lord?

Some translations even say that the Spirit "compelled" or "drove" Jesus into the wilderness.

Does Your Spirit have a purpose for me here in the wilderness?

A beauty emerges from a life that has endured many difficult in-betweens. May we live, love, laugh, and weep through all these seasons. But for now, let's struggle through the in-between season and hold on to truths God has given us.

9

The Valley of Decision

In the book of Joel, the prophet warned the people to turn to God. A final judgment was coming, he warned. He called it the "day of the Lord." He said in that day the sun and moon will be darkened. The Lord will roar from Zion and thunder from Jerusalem. Earth and sky will tremble. But the Lord will be the refuge for his people.

Doesn't that second-coming vision sound a lot like the day Jesus died? The day He was crucified, the sun was darkened, and Jesus let out a loud cry, "It is finished." Then the earth shook and rocks were torn asunder. He died to pay the ransom for us that we may find refuge in Him.

Chapter 3 of Joel speaks about "multitudes, multitudes in the valley of decision! For the day of the Lord is near in the valley of decision."

I love how that phrase flows through my mind. The *valley of decision*. What choice will you make in your valley of decision? Throughout this book, we'll ponder the choices we must make. Here in the in-between, in the wilderness valley, choices are important. The choice you make in the valley determines the view you will have on the mountaintop as you look forward toward your destination.

10

Swamp Creatures

Whenever I write of traversing valleys, my thoughts immediately go back to the treacherous swamp crossings on my Appalachian Trail hike. The White Mountains in New Hampshire offered the most awe-inspiring, breathtaking mountaintop experiences of the entire trail; yet in the valleys between, we encountered some of the most treacherous landscapes.

I was so close to entering Maine, the fourteenth and final state of my hike. Only two more miles to go. But those miles were over the swampy terrain of marshy sags. Sags are lower areas between two mountains. In one particular area, the bogs were the result of centuries of decay—trees, vegetation, insects, and undoubtedly even larger animals had died and, covered with water that collected there, created a primordial soup.

Rain had fallen for days as I hiked, and in many places narrow wooden boards put down to aid in crossing the bogs were now under water. I cautiously started across one bog, tapping my hiking sticks on the submerged boards, seeking purchase for my feet.

Dear God, protect me, I prayed. That soup looked as though it were yearning for a human ingredient.

Suddenly one hiking stick slipped off the edge of a board. I lost my balance, and with a loud cry to God for help, I tumbled into the murky depths where there was no foothold.

Sound familiar?

You've read about this in Psalms 69. David's tumble into a swamp sounds similar to my fall: "Save me, oh God, for the waters have come up to my neck. I sink in the miry depths where there is no foothold. I have come into the deep waters; the floods engulf me."

Have you ever been up to your neck in despair? Have you ever felt like there is no foothold beneath you? It's a miserable place to be, isn't it? Psalm 69 accurately describes it in painful detail.

David pleads with God. "Do not hide your face from your servant, answer me quickly, for I am in trouble. I am in pain and distress. May your salvation, oh God, protect me."

We get stuck in swamps in the valleys for a variety of reasons. Many times, circumstances are beyond our control. Other times, we are in the swamp because we've made bad choices.

The first thing to do is to cry out to God for help.

"God, help me!" I screamed. "I'm sinking!" The waters were coming up to my neck. I grabbed for the unsteady board and slowly extricated myself from the miry depths. I was a swamp creature covered in muck when I finally emerged.

There is no foothold when we venture or are dumped into the swamps of life. David, writer of many of the psalms, cried out for help many times. In the last few months, I've found that many of David's words express my feelings and situation exactly. I've gone back to the book of Psalms again and again.

Like David, when we're sinking in the swamp, we need a solid rock to stand on. That rock is Jesus. God offers salvation. Rescue.

> And the God of all grace, who called you to His eternal glory in Christ, after you have suffered a little while, will himself restore you and make you strong, firm and steadfast. (1 Peter 5:10)

Peter knew something about falling in swamps; I'm sure he agonized through in-between days, the days between the moment he betrayed his friendship with Jesus and the morning on the beach when Jesus reassured Peter he was forgiven and loved. Peter was changed by his suffering. His letter written later in life gives us this promise: God does restore our strength and places our feet on solid footing once again.

I was covered with slime and mud as I crawled out of the bog. When I came to a stream, I jumped into the water and let it flow over me and wash off the dead, stagnant muck.

That's what Jesus does for us. We often need a cleansing. He provides pure, spiritual, living water to wash off the muck and revive us. It's the water of life that only He can provide.

Know that Jesus will walk with you through the in-betweens. The suffering will come to an end. God will rescue you and then wash and cleanse you when you lose your foothold and the waters of the swamp are up to your neck.

11

"Trust Me"

Following my plummet from the pedestal to the living stone, my mind was often thrown into turmoil with troubled thoughts.

Had I been blind to some obvious obstacles?

Only after the dismissed guard returned did he make it clear that yes, I missed many signs. Of course, my Guard and Guide had been with me all along, but I was willingly deaf to any warnings. Had I listened earlier to the Holy Spirit, He would have saved me from so much pain and misery. With His guidance now, I can easily go back to places and incidents during those two years where the truth would have been apparent—had I been more aware.

My thoughts paralyzed any attempt at recovery from grief, but I needed to figure things out. It's just how my mind works. Some folks can function even if they're only given half-truths. Not me. I spent many daylight hours and sleepless nights trying to put together all the pieces of the puzzle. My mind staggered through the countless questions of *Why? How could my best friend do this to me?*

36 DON'T WAIT **TOO LONG**

In Psalms 55, David cries out to God. "My thoughts trouble me, and I am distraught." He goes on to speak about his fear, anguish, suffering, and distress. He even wishes for dove's wings to escape the pain, to fly away and be at rest.

Yet the very last line of the psalm is this: "But as for me, I trust in you."

This is one of David's statements that I've now used countless times in the clutches of my own distress. At times, this is the only thing I can say to God: "I'm trusting You."

How about you? In your hurts and pain, are you able to say "But as for me, God, I trust in you"?

We can trust God in every aspect of our lives. Often when we talk of trusting Him, we are referring to the events and direction of our lives. But we can trust Him with our inner life, too. Those thoughts that we can't seem to control can throw us into turmoil and twist and color all of our perspective. Just as we can trust God for healing of our deepest wounds, we can trust Him with our thoughts and feelings.

Paul has words of advice for us:

> Finally, brothers and sisters, whatever is true, whatever is noble, whatever is right, whatever is pure, whatever is lovely, whatever is admirable—if anything is excellent or praiseworthy—think about such things. (Philippians 4:8)

Are you troubled by thoughts that only leave you in distress and turmoil? Ask God to help you replace them with thoughts within these guidelines. Ask Him to give you that peace that transcends all understanding and stands guard over your heart and mind. (See Philippians 4:7)

His peace is a miraculous peace.

12

So Lonely, I Cried

    I'm sure a few of you recognized the similarity of the above title to an old Hank Williams tune. A line in that song envisions the moon going behind a cloud so it could cry in its lonely and solitary place.
    Loss of a close relationship, whether from death or breakup, can result in devastating loneliness. The excruciating pain of aloneness is so intense you can almost taste it. Have you ever been so lonesome you cried? I have, and I did.
    Following my breakup, there were times I entered my house and felt intense loneliness. I'm convinced the devil takes advantage of people going through the emotional wilderness of loneliness. A spiritual battle raged in my mind. I fought thoughts such as *You're worthless. You're alone because you're not good enough. No one wants you.* If you have a friend who is a prayer warrior, don't hesitate to call them when you're fighting those horrible thoughts. I have a friend I called several times. Prayer always made a difference in the battle.

38 DON'T WAIT **TOO LONG**

I'm writing this now because I just had a battle with the loneliness demon this evening. It's a Saturday evening. From my perspective, everyone else is out enjoying life as happy couples. I sit alone at home, crying in sadness and aloneness.

Besides prayer, what can we do to combat these thoughts? I went to Psalms to see what my friend David would say to me. David and I have grown close over the last few months. We are both men after God's own heart. We love greatly, and we fail greatly. Why God chooses to still love us is a bit of a mystery... but He does.

So, I found my way to Psalms 25 on this tearful Saturday night.

To you, O Lord, I lift up my soul. I put my trust in you, says David.

The soul is the real us. It's the part of us that lives after our body dies. Our souls go to Heaven and await a reuniting with our new bodies.

Imagine the arms of your soul reaching heavenward. Imagine your outstretched, longing soul praising God and saying "I trust in You."

Do you ever get impatient with God? Have you prayed and prayed for or about someone? You're convinced it is an honorable prayer. You trusted and believed the verses about asking what you will and God will grant it. And yet, nothing happens. Only silence. And crickets chirping.

How long, oh God, how long?

David prayed for God to show him the right way. He wanted truth; he wanted to be taught; he wanted to follow the right way. All day long, David had hope. (Sometimes my hope is minute by minute.)

David's hope included the desire that God had forgotten his youthful sins and rebellious ways. Yes, I enjoy the same hope about my sins and rebellious ways.

Verse 9 says, "[God] guides the humble in what is right, and teaches them His way."

God, I pray for humility. I want to be taught.

In verse 16, David speaks my language. I could have written the next three verses. If you, like I, suffer loneliness from a loss, you will read these verses differently than someone "being carried to the skies on flowery beds of ease."

That's a phrase from an old hymn we used to sing in church, "Am I a Soldier of the Cross." But you, like me, are probably feeling more like the next lines in that hymn, like those who have "fought to win the prize and sailed through bloody seas." (You're learning some trivia tonight. Trivia through tears. Oh yes, back to those verses David penned about *my* state of heart and mind.)

> Turn to me and be gracious to me, for I am lonely and afflicted. The troubles of my heart have multiplied, free me from my anguish. Look upon my affliction and my distress and take away all my sins. (Psalm 25:16-18)

David wrote my thoughts and feelings better than I could—except for the request to take away my sins. I know the record against me is already canceled.

David also speaks about his enemies increasing. His enemies were dangerous. His life was in danger. I doubt any of our lives are in that kind of jeopardy. However, it would be good to look at our lives and recognize things that are hindering our spiritual growth. Jesus warned us about enemies who can kill the soul, even more dangerous than the enemies tracking down David. Our enemy uses our thoughts and emotions spawned by loneliness.

What keeps us from escaping our loneliness? What keeps us stuck there? Why is the battle so long?

If I had all those answers, I wouldn't have been crying alone at home tonight. The one thing I do know is that by digging into God's Word with David, I do feel better. That's what friends do. Thanks, David. We will talk more.

David concludes this chapter by making a statement I've also adopted for my own use over the past lonely months.

"God, my hope is in You."

My best advice to anyone going through such a period of intense loneliness is this: Allow your mind to be open to hearing from God. He actually does love you and does care about you. The process may require a bit of patience, too. I have a short supply of that right now, but there's no shortcut or easy way through aloneness. Seek out a mentor or a teacher who is willing to help.

Offer your hurts to God, and trust Him.

Don't wait too long!

13

The Alabaster Heart

She was troubled. In pain. Within her lived a deep longing for peace, but peace was elusive. A life of sin had built walls around her heart that no kindness could penetrate.

We are told by Jesus in Luke 7:47 that she had many sins. Although her sins are not specified, she was likely a prostitute.

Had men used and abused her heart? The walls now kept them all out. No man could speak words that had the power to puncture her guarding walls. But then, no man in her sphere of sinning had ever tried.

Those walls around her heart also held everything in, held back the pain, anger, abuse, deceit, and shame of many years. Her heart was a reservoir filled with tears that needed release. Could the dam holding back those tears ever be cracked and broken open? Would the breaking open be too painful to even consider?

Her pain and shame held tightly to the walls around her heart. Would she even want anyone to break through? Then she would have to address the wounds and remorse she felt. Could she even be that vulnerable?

There was no hope for her. Sinning with others was her only value. Her mind often numbed her heart, banishing feeling, allowing her to survive another day.

Then she met hope.

Perhaps she heard Jesus teach one day. Maybe she was traversing between sins when she heard the teacher. Had she heard Jesus teach about forgiveness? Had she glimpsed hope in words He spoke? Some encounter must have occurred to give her the desire and courage to barge into Simon the Pharisee's house when he had guests.

We are not told how or even what she knew of Jesus. However, something caused little fissures to form in those walls.

She had one chance to change her life. She either cleaned up her life of sin, or faced a lifetime of misery. She knew it was now or never. The fissures started to crack. The cracks expanded. The dam was about to burst.

The promise of peace and healing was worth the risk of embarrassment.

But first she needed to retrieve that alabaster vase containing the valuable perfume. She often looked at that beautiful, translucent vase in her house. It had great value to her. Was it a gift from a loved one, or for her own use to entice sinners?

The perfume vase was most likely produced in Egypt in a town named Alabastron. There, lime formed on the floors of limestone caves; and over the centuries, water seeped through the limestone, giving it a matchless translucence. Boxes, jars, and vases produced from this mineral seemed to glow from the inside out.

She had heard that the teacher of hope and forgiveness would be at Simon the Pharisee's house for dinner. I wonder if she questioned why Jesus would visit the house of a Pharisee, much less eat with him.

Clutching her alabaster vase, she did what less sinful women in that town were unwilling to do. She invited herself.

She did what we are all permitted to do. She approached Jesus boldly.

A sinner, a savior, and Simon. This was not the situation Simon had envisioned when he invited Jesus for dinner. In reality, two sinners and a savior met that night.

The cracks around the sinful woman's heart broke open. The walls could no longer contain the tears stored up for so many years. Pain and anguish, fear and regrets were washed away by the streams of tears pouring out of the vase of her heart.

She knelt before the savior and wept her tears of regret and remorse. Her sins washed over the feet of Jesus as she baptized His feet. And as the tear-stained sins touched Jesus' feet, they were forgiven. The risk she had taken was worth the reward of peace and contentment.

Peace and freedom and love now rushed in to fill the empty chamber of her alabaster heart. She grasped her long flowing hair in her hands and gently wiped Jesus' feet. In complete humility, she kissed His feet and then reached for the alabaster vase. Weeping, she broke open the neck of the vase and anointed Jesus' feet with expensive perfume mixed with tears.

We are not told of any words exchanged.

Simon, however, was not pleased with what was taking place. In his mind, a skunk had just invaded his garden party.

He muttered under his breath, "If he actually is a prophet, he would surely know what kind of woman this is. She is a sinner, and she's touching him!"

However, among those three, only one sinner remained. The woman had been redeemed.

We are told of the words that pass between Jesus and Simon.

"Simon," Jesus said, "I have something to say to you."

"Yes?"

"A man lends money to two people. One gets a loan for 500 denarii, while the other gets 50 denarii. Of course, the man wants to be paid back, but both these borrowers are flat broke. They can't pay their debt. As an act of kindness, the lender forgives both loans.

"Now, Simon, who do you think will love that lender more? The man who owed a huge debt, or the man who owned a small one?"

Simon might have suspected a trick question, but he answered that it was probably the one with the larger debt.

"You are correct, Simon." Jesus now faced the woman but spoke to Simon. "Simon, I'm a guest in your house, and it's your responsibility to provide water to wash my feet. You didn't. She washed my feet with her tears and dried them with her hair. I entered your house, and you didn't greet me with a customary kiss. This woman washed, dried, and kissed my feet. Finally, you neglected to put oil on my head, but she has poured out her expensive perfume on my feet.

"Simon, this woman had sins that were the equivalent of 500 denarii. It was a crushing debt. Repayment was impossible. The love she has shown me is why I'm canceling her debt; therefore, all her sins are forgiven."

Jesus was still looking at her as He spoke to Simon. He then addressed the woman. "Your sins are forgiven. Your faith had saved you. Go in peace."

Her alabaster heart had at last been broken open. Walls holding in sin and inhibiting goodness had been demolished. Tears now were tears of joy, tears of hope.

Friend, do walls of pain encircle your heart? Have the courage to come boldly to the one who can destroy strongholds. Hear those healing words, "Your faith has saved you." Find peace.

If Jesus has already canceled your debt and healed you, is your life as transparent as an alabaster vase? Does the love of Jesus shine from within you? Are you willing to be poured out on some person in need of compassion? When the perfume poured out on Jesus' feet, the vase was emptied. Your alabaster heart, however, is an artesian heart. As quickly as you let love flow out, Jesus will fill it back up again. Pour out. Be filled!

Break open the alabaster heart within you.

The aroma of that expensive perfume filled Simon's house long after the woman left. May our love and compassion also leave a lingering aroma long after we're gone.

14

Come and See

The book of John is my favorite of the four Gospels. John gives us so much to see, read, feel, and discover about following Jesus.

"In the beginning..." The first three words of the first verse already give me reason to pause and ponder—and there are still twenty-one more words to go.

God always *was*. My mind is boggled at that. God existed in eternity past and will exist in eternity future. Before anything existed, there was the Word.

Word.

Words have meaning. All those billions and billions of thoughts wrapped up in God and called *Word*, all this knowledge and wisdom becoming flesh when Jesus was born. I can only comprehend the simplest part of that: Jesus was born. Being born is a common experience for humanity. But believing He was born to a virgin? Yes, accepting that requires faith.

You see how the book of John sets my mind to working in many directions. I began this chapter, intending to write about John the Baptist (who, by the way, is not the same "John" who wrote the Gospel). But already we've detoured.

Back to the first chapter of the book of John, where we meet John the Baptist. He was sent by God to tell everyone that God was sending a light, a light that would give life to everyone.

John was living out in the wilderness, preaching and baptizing. One day, his cousin Jesus was in the crowd of people who came to hear him. Unbeknownst to the baptizer, the person he had been preaching about was there, listening to his words. John the writer reports that John the baptizer did not realize Jesus was the One, the Word, the Messiah.

I find it amazing that John did not know there was something special about his cousin until Jesus asked to be baptized and walked into the water like many others had done. Then the heavens opened and the baptizer saw the Holy Spirit coming down and resting on Jesus. It was a Great Reveal. This was the sign that Jesus was the Chosen One of God.

In the three other gospels, we learn that the Holy Spirit then led Jesus into the wilderness where Jesus was grilled and tested to the extreme by the devil. He passed the test with flying colors and was ready to start His teaching ministry. The final act in God's plan was Jesus' death, His resurrection, and His becoming the way through which we find peace with God. It's a brilliant plan.

John the Baptist had several disciples who were curious about Jesus. Later, they approached Him, and asked Him where He was staying. A simple question, but Jesus answered with these life-changing words:

"Come, and you will see."

That is the invitation for you or anyone wanting to know where Jesus is and who Jesus is. The Gospel of John is a doorway you can enter to find answers and the path to a changed life. Take the risk of discovering the truth. Like the woman with the alabaster heart, you will find peace and contentment are worth the risk. The doorway has the welcome mat out: Come to the book of John, come meet Jesus, and you will see.

If you are unsure of your relationship with Jesus and too much of your life is pretending, the book of John will set you right if you allow it. You will exit John a new creature. Your life will be changed, your soul cleansed, and you will enter a new chapter in your life. A chapter where your acts will be honorable to God, family, and community.

What are you waiting for?

You've already waited too long!

Come and see!

15

Jesus, the Forsaken Scapegoat

Imagine that there is some sin in your life. Big or little, major or minor, it doesn't matter. Sin is sin in God's eyes. You know you have transgressed God's laws. You know you need to somehow be cleansed of that sin. It's a great burden on your mind and your heart, it's keeping you awake at night, and it's suffocating your conscience. What to do about all that guilt?

I am so thankful we no longer live under Old Testament law. If we did, getting rid of that guilt and shame would be much more inconvenient—and to do so, you might even have to wait a year!

Finally, when the one day of forgiveness does arrive, you'll travel to your local livestock auction (or to your own herds), and pick out two goats. One goat will be sacrificed; its blood will cleanse your church. The second goat will transport your sins away on its head. The question of which goat is more fortunate is open for debate. One dies; the other one lives, but is the scapegoat and is sent off into exile and condemnation.

50 DON'T WAIT **TOO LONG**

In Leviticus 16, we read God's instructions for the Day of Atonement, the one day when folks could be cleansed of their sins. The ceremonies at the tabernacle involved at least fifteen rituals the high priest had to perform to cleanse himself and the tabernacle first, and then to rid the children of Israel of their sins. There was a copious amount of animal bloodshed, plenty of animal sacrifices, and instructions on the precise priestly garments to wear. Everything had to be done according to detailed instructions. Deliberate and elaborate, the symbolism all pointed to a permanent sacrifice yet to come, one that would be made "once for all time" (Hebrews 10:10).

Two young, perfect goats were chosen and lots were cast to determine the fate of each of these kids. One goat was chosen to die, and its blood was sprinkled on the mercy seat in the Holy of Holies. This act cleansed the Most Holy Place from the sins of Israel. This blood also represented the future death of Jesus and the shedding of His blood.

However, the sins still remained, a stain on the people. It was time for the scapegoat to take its place.

Have you ever been a scapegoat? A scapegoat gets the blame for something someone else did. It takes responsibility for whatever wrong was done by another person.

The high priest took that goat and put his hands on its head and confessed the sins of the people. All the sins were loaded on that one head. A designated man drove the goat out into the wilderness, ten miles into the desert. They didn't want that sin-laden goat returning to camp!

Imagine coming to the ceremonies that day, sick with guilt. You've carried the burden so long. It's affected your health and your relationships, and you cringe when you think of God looking over the camp and His eyes coming to rest on you...

But finally, you will be rid of that shame. You watch as the goat carrying the guilt of your transgression disappears off in the distance. Finally! What a relief!

Then you go home. And before the next day is over, you have already lost your temper with your aged, cranky father, lied to your brother, or coveted the fancy tent next door. Oh, and before you could catch it, an oath slipped out in anger. Within twenty-four hours, you've already broken almost half of the Ten Commandments! Guilt creeps back in. God must be so angry with you.

There just has to be a better way.

There is. God found a scapegoat to take on the sins of humanity. Your sins. My sins. One sacrifice, for all time. Jesus hung on a cross one day, and on His head, God put all the sins of all humanity of all time. Jesus was the final sacrifice for all our sins *and* the one who carried them all away.

Can you imagine the horror that God felt as he looked down upon that scene? There was His beloved Son, crushed under the burden of sin. It was such a ghastly sight that God had to turn away for a short period of time.

My God, My God, why have you forsaken me?

God did not abandon Jesus; God did not reject Him; He was forsaken until the sacrifice was complete.

God cannot tolerate sin. God and sin cannot coexist. For a period of time, God banished Jesus from the presence of the Most Holy God.

That separation from God is what we deserved, but Jesus endured that separation for us. Can you imagine His anguish as He felt His Father turn away from Him, as He was driven into a wilderness?

He became our scapegoat, and on that day, Jesus became the final remedy for the sin disease.

16

Self-Judgment

If you ever commit some type of transgression and have a court date to appear in front of a judge, his decision will be final. You will have a chance to make your case, or perhaps a counselor will make it for you. But it will be the judge who declares the verdict. Then you'll pay the fine, go to jail, or if you're fortunate, perhaps go free.

Can you imagine going to court and being told you will be judging yourself? The judge will be silent. You will speak, and your words will either convict you or set you free.

Now take this scene out of your imagination and know that it will be a reality. Yes, we will stand in front of a judge someday. And our destination will be determined by our own words.

This warning comes from Jesus.

He had just healed a demon-possessed man. The Pharisees heard about it and began their accusations, saying Jesus was casting out demons by the power of Beelzebub, the prince of demons. Jesus pointed out the ridiculousness of their criticism: If Satan works against Satan, his kingdom will soon fall.

Jesus went on to shine the light on their problem: A good tree produces good fruit. A bad tree will have bad fruit. Out of the evil in the heart comes evil fruit. Out of the goodness of a heart comes good fruit. The Pharisees had a treasury of evil stored up in their hearts.

Then Jesus got really serious with them. His words are also a very serious warning for us, a warning about the power of words spoken.

I've often written about the power of words. That's one of the things I learned on the Appalachian Trail, and now I see it constantly in daily living and in the responses I get to my written words. Our words have so much more power than we even imagine.

We'll be held accountable for how we wield that power. Every person will give their account on the day of judgment. We'll have to give an account for every careless word we have spoken. And it's not the words you *wish* you had said. It's the words that you have already spoken during your lifetime.

I used to wonder how God could possibly store every word. But with our modern technology, we can now record and keep track of almost everything. Millions of bits of information are available at our fingertips. If man can do that, God certainly doesn't have a problem keeping track of our words.

"By your words you will be acquitted, and by your words you will be condemned," Jesus said (Matthew 12:37). I believe there will be little doubt, and each of us will quickly realize what the verdict will be.

I hope that when my time comes and my words are judging me, no one nearby overhears the list of words and deeds for which I'll need to give account. *You did that? You said that?* they may think or even say.

Yes, that's right. I said it. I did it.

But wait. The good part is still coming. There are powerful words yet to be heard. Words with meaning that will seal my future.

Hear them: "Jesus, I believe. Remember me. Forgive me. I want to be in You and You in me."

I will have judged myself. Acquitted!

Then I will hear those words I've waited and lived for: "I commend you for your faith. Welcome home. Your race is done."

Now, my dear reader, don't underestimate the power of words. Yes, words have meaning. Those words you choose to say will determine your future eternal destination.

Chose to say those powerful words that lead to an eternity with Jesus.

Don't wait too long.

Jesus, the Curtain

By the time of Jesus, the tent tabernacle of the wilderness had been replaced by a building, the temple built in Jerusalem. The layout was the same as that of the tabernacle.

The curtain walling off the Most Holy Place was thick, heavy, and high—thirty feet high and sixty feet long. Behind that curtain was the Ark of the Covenant, a box holding Aaron's rod that had miraculously budded, a jar of manna, and the stone tablets on which God had written His ten commandments. These items had great significance to the journey of the Israelites. On top of the Ark was the mercy seat, where God would appear in a cloud.

The Most Holy Place (or the Holy of Holies, as it is sometimes called) was the place of God's presence. Common priests were permitted to come every day to burn incense on the golden altar in the area outside the curtain, but only the high priest could go into the actual presence of God, and then only one time a year, following the instructions God had given for the Day of Atonement. As Aaron's two sons learned, it was very dangerous to enter there if not following precise directives for admittance. Leviticus 10 gives the account of their offering unauthorized fire before the Lord. They had not followed guidelines, and authorized fire came from the presence of God and killed them.

That curtain was the dividing line between life and death for all but the high priest—and he, too, had to be "perfect" in his approach to God.

The moment Jesus died, a great sound was heard in the temple. That curtain separating everyone from God's presence was torn in two, ripped from top bottom. God tore the curtain apart and issued an open invitation to humanity: Enter this Most Holy Place and draw near to God. Come into God's presence.

Yes, that's true! We don't have to feel timid or unworthy. Paul writes in Hebrews that we're to come "confidently" and "boldly."

What happened? What is different now?

Christ died to give us the privilege of entering God's presence. He opened a "new and life-giving way" (Hebrews 10:20). There is no longer a barrier between us and our Creator God.

Hebrews uses two other illustrations to describe what Jesus did for us. Jesus is called our high priest; He is the one who went to God on our behalf. He is also called the curtain. We walk through Him to enter God's presence. Jesus is the only way; He is the dividing line between life and death. With the way opened by His blood, we are free to enter at any time.

The writer of Hebrews explains it:

> But when Christ came as high priest of the good things that are now already here, He went through the greater and more perfect tabernacle that is not

man-made, that is to say not a part of this creation. He did not enter by means of the blood of goats and calves, but He entered the Most Holy Place once for all by His own blood, having obtained eternal redemption. (Hebrews 9:11-12)

The Most Holy Place awaits you. Walk through that divided curtain and meet Jesus by the mercy seat. Again, Hebrews tells us what we can expect: We will "receive mercy and find grace to help us in our time of need." Bring your troubled, in-between soul there.

Don't wait.

18

The Yoke's on You

A yoke. What picture does that bring to your mind?

We typically think of a yoke as that wooden collar that keeps two animals like oxen connected to each other and working together. I would have loved to have a team of oxen carrying my burden of a backpack on the Appalachian Trail. Every morning, I packed it up and picked it up, burdening my shoulders, my legs, my entire body. I couldn't hand it off to anyone else. I was stuck with it for 2,176 miles. There were days when Jesus' words about being "weary and heavy laden" were all too true of me.

Jesus tells us the answer to the burdens we bear is to go to Him and take His yoke upon us. Voluntarily?

Here's a misconception my youthful mind got stuck on: I used to think that if I was yoked to Jesus, I would be burdened with tasks He required of me or a long list of forbidden pleasures in life.

But no! It turns out that Jesus' words in Matthew 11 verses 28 and 29 are words of comfort for troubled and weary souls.

"My yoke is easy," He says. "I am gentle and humble in heart. Come to me, and I'll give you rest."

That sounds quite the opposite of carrying a heavy burden. Jesus assures us He will be carrying all the weight. We are tethered to Him to allow His love to give us sweet rest from our hurts and pains.

Perhaps we are yoked to our sinful nature. We're carrying burdens of guilt and remorse. Paul writes in Galatians 5 verse 1 that Christ set us free from a yoke of slavery to sin. That's where we were before Christ offered us His rest and freedom.

It might sound strange to talk of freedom and yokes at the same time, but let's be honest: Whether we are on the narrow pathway that leads to eternal life or on the broad road leading to everlasting death, we travel the road yoked to our guide. We will arrive at that destination eternally yoked to the same guide. The guide on the broad road isn't concerned with helping you carry your load of guilt and pain. He seeks to continue adding to that burden. The guide on the narrow road, however, *has already* carried it off for you.

A good description of being yoked to Jesus is found in John 15. Jesus says, "I'm the vine; you're a branch." Many times in Scripture, Jesus says "Remain in me, and I in you. We can get through this together if you only stay connected to me."

From what is Jesus offering to give you rest? Hurts from a failed relationship? Loss of a loved one? The wounds of betrayal inflicted by a trusted friend? Guilt? Regrets?

Traveling on our own, we carry back-breaking burdens. Jesus says, "Give it to Me. I'll carry that for you so that you can rest."

Why carry that burden alone? Go to Him and let Him attach you securely to Himself and relieve you of the encumbrance.

Don't wait too long. Don't you need a rest?

19

"Lord, Save Me!"

Those words were uttered by two people on two different bodies of water, both caught in a storm. One man was named Peter; the other, Paul. Peter was on the Sea of Galilee; I was on a lake in Minnesota. We were both in deep peril.

Fortunately for Peter and the other disciples, Jesus was up on a mountainside praying and saw the boat buffeted by the wind when it was a considerable distance from land.

I'm getting way ahead of my story. Let's go back to the beginning of this long, hard day for Jesus.

This day started with Jesus receiving devastating news. His cousin had just lost his head. He didn't lose his head figuratively, but literally. The governor, Herod, had just put John the Baptist to death by beheading.

The news of John's death caused Jesus to seek a solitary place to pray. This was not unusual for Jesus. He often went to a solitary place when He needed to talk to God. I can certainly imagine that Jesus might have questioned why God would allow John's death.

What was unusual was how Jesus chose to find that solitary place to pray. He went by boat. Alone.

Isn't that amazing? The account is in Matthew 14. When Jesus heard what had happened to his cousin, He withdrew by boat privately to a solitary place. Imagine that. Jesus in a fishing boat that was capable of carrying Him and the disciples, and He was rowing it by Himself.

He needed to be alone with His Father God.

However, while Jesus was on the water seeking that solitary place, crowds saw the direction He was heading and followed on foot. When Jesus landed His craft, the crowd was already there, waiting for Him. Instead of retreating to pray, He took compassion on them and healed the folks who were sick.

Toward evening, the disciples finally caught up with Jesus and reminded Him that He had, indeed, found a place so remote that the crowd would need to go to surrounding villages to find supper.

"Why don't you just feed them," Jesus replied.

We all know how that all-you-can-eat buffet worked out.

Five thousand men plus women and children were fed that day. I managed a restaurant for many years, and feeding 5,000 at our restaurant made for a very busy day for our staff. I know the preparations and the help necessary to feed that many. I know about ordering food and food preparation. I know about grill lines, buffet lines, clearing tables, and washing dishes.

I also know that to make money in food service, a manager needs to control food and labor costs. For Jesus, the food costs ran to five loaves and two fish, and labor costs were zero.

Imagine me walking into the restaurant kitchen and giving the kitchen prep cooks two fish and five loaves of bread.

"Listen up, cooks. Here's today's food delivery. And we'll likely have over 10,000 guests to feed." They would look at me and say, "Do you expect us to do miracles?"

Jesus took the food and gave it to the twelve disciples, and they fed the crowd. On days when our crew fed 5,000 guests, we needed thirteen hours, from 7:00 AM to 8:00 PM, and at least eighty workers to accomplish that. Those days were long days that demanded everything of us and left us depleted.

It had been a difficult, depleting day for Jesus, too. The end of the long day finally came. Before the crowd had even dispersed, Jesus told His disciples they could call it a day and take the boat back home. One wonders how late it was until the last of the thousands had gone and Jesus was finally alone.

We aren't told exactly where Jesus had landed in His attempt to find time alone with God, but we do know there was a mountain there, and Jesus went up on the mountain to finally have His time with His Father.

Even then, He had His eye on His disciples. The boat was already a good distance away when Jesus saw a storm had hit and His friends were in peril.

Jesus went for a walk. He walked out to them. On the water.

Put yourself in the boat with the disciples. They've had a long, hard day, and they've been up all night. Now this storm is draining the last ounces of their energy. Then, out of the gloom of the storm, they think they see a figure out on the water. *On* the water.

They freak out. Fear overcomes them. They believe they are seeing a ghost. What else could it be but a supernatural being?

And then, they hear the words, "It's me. Don't be afraid."

I suppose they are all startled to hear Peter speak up. Maybe even Peter is shocked to hear the words coming out of his mouth.

"Jesus, if that's really you, tell me to leave the boat and walk towards you," calls Peter.

"Come."

You know the story. Peter walked on water—until his eyes were drawn to the churning waves and his thoughts focused again on the storm. Then he began to sink, and he cried out, "Lord, save me!"

I know you've been hit broadside by storms. It has happened or will happen to all of us. You see no possible way to weather the storm. It's almost impossible to navigate. You aren't making any headway; you're just trying to keep from drowning.

I know how it feels to be fighting for life in such a storm. I can't for the life of me imagine why Peter (or I) would say, "Okay, Jesus, if you're really there, tell me to get out of this boat and walk on water."

We tend to think that staying in the boat is the surest way to survive. We just want to get through this really dark, discouraging night and get on with life.

But what happens when Jesus asks even more of you? When He asks you to do what seems impossible? And what if He asks when you are already in the middle of a storm?

Jesus seems to be saying to you, "Trust Me. Step out of the boat. Have the courage to walk towards me."

Could you? Can you?

Can you trust Jesus to keep you from sinking?

As you contemplate that step of faith, hear what Jesus is saying to you.

"Take courage, it is I. Don't be afraid. Come."

20

"Lord, Save Me, Too!"

A bicycle ride across America took me across the Mississippi River in Cairo, Illinois. I paused on the bridge, admiring the huge barges heading downriver. *Someday, I'd like to kayak the entire Mississippi River*, I mused.

And that is how many of my adventures began. With a thought, which turned into an idea, which turned into a plan.

Gathering maps, information, and equipment, I saw an ad for a sea kayak. I had no idea what the difference was between a sea kayak and any other kayak, but the deal looked good. The seller was in Chicago; a friend drove me there, we strapped the sea kayak onto the roof of the car, and we brought it home.

Later in the summer, the same friend transported me to Minnesota, where the headwaters of the Mississippi are barely six inches deep and laze along as a calm little creek. The kayak and I floated away—to a misery I'd never imagined. Before the first day was over, I was in the clutches of the river's swamps, fighting my way through weeds and brush.

After the swamps, the Mississippi flows through several lakes. When I finally escaped the weeds, I had to cross these lakes and then navigate twenty-seven locks before I'd get to what I thought would be clear sailing down the Mississippi.

I crossed two smaller lakes successfully. A larger one loomed ahead. Cass Lake is ten miles long and seven miles wide and has a rare distinction. In the middle of the lake is an island with a lake in the middle.

My guidebook advised that crossing Cass Lake (as opposed to getting to the other side by skirting it and staying close to shore) could be treacherous. Winds came up quickly and were dangerous. But I was paddling through the neighborhood, and who wouldn't want to see this unusual lake-on-an-island-in-a-lake?

My plan was to make the three-mile crossing to the island, tent for the night, visit the other lake, and the next day paddle the remaining four miles to the other side of Cass Lake and go on my merry way down the Mississippi.

The waters were calm when I started my paddle to Star Island, but that quickly changed when I'd covered about half the distance. Out of nowhere, menacing five-foot waves came rolling toward me.

Fortunately, I had a *sea* kayak. The construction of the sea kayak was just what was needed in the waves of Cass Lake. The kayak had a rudder and foot pedals that allowed me to steer into the waves. In the swamps, I was unable to use the rudder since the water was so shallow the rudder would have acted like a plow. But on the lake, the rudder was essential. The kayak also had a spray skirt, which is a tarp that attaches to the craft and covers the open areas of the kayak so that water washes over the skirt rather than falling into and filling up the cockpit.

The waves did wash over me. I paddled furiously and prayed diligently. I paddled until blisters formed on my hands. I have never been so afraid of losing my life as that day. Not during the tornado on the Appalachian Trail; not throughout that long, lonely night when I crossed the mountains on my bike with barely any light; not on the highways when the heavy traffic could have squashed me like a bug.

I was paddling diagonally to the island, and I knew I needed to make the turn towards shore. Slamming my foot pedal in the direction I needed to turn, I screamed, "Lord, save me!"

Jesus was not sleeping in the front of my boat. He did not come walking on the water to save me. Fortunately, He didn't ask me to leave the boat, either.

However, Jesus was watching over me.

As I turned toward shore, I saw the large wave approaching from the side, and I knew this would be the wave that overturned my kayak and drowned me. *This is it. This is the moment I'm going to die.*

Instead, it turned out to be the thrill ride of my life. That wave swooped under my kayak to pick it up and toss it, but the kayak rolled right over that wave "like a boss." And it turned me in the direction of the shore.

The waves now hitting me from behind hastened my approach to shore. At last, my craft ground upon the sandy beach. Trembling and shaking, I climbed out of the kayak and fell to the ground, kissing the beach. Sand never tasted so good.

Thank you, Jesus!

I was safe, at least for the night. I did realize I was only three miles across a seven-mile lake. My brain did function enough to remind me that I had a four-mile crossing the following day.

I had no idea, though, that in a few days, amazing events would unfold.

Events that only God could orchestrate.

21

Saved and Rescued

Most of the time, my plans for adventure worked. The plan to kayak the Mississippi did not.

My plan didn't work for the same reason Jonah's plan didn't work. Jonah was going the wrong direction. He was not working the plan God had shown him. I was going in the wrong direction, too, but at least God didn't stuff me into the belly of the whale for three days. Instead, I was swallowed up by weeds and rice paddies and terrifying lake winds before God rescued me.

You'll need to know a bit of the backstory.

As I made plans for that kayak trip, I was offered two other opportunities for the summer. One was a bus trip with my cousins. This is a yearly tradition, and in that particular year, the trip was going to visit several national parks in the West and also go up into Banff National Park in Canada. Of course I wanted to go, but they were scheduled to depart shortly before I was headed to the headwaters of the Mississippi, and they would not be back before I would set sail. I wavered a bit, but in the end stuck to my plan for the kayaking trip.

I was also asked to write the life story of a successful local businessman. He'd been diagnosed with cancer, and the prognosis was grim. I turned down the opportunity. I was going to paddle the Mississippi River. God and I never discussed either one of these options. I had my plan. I wasn't listening to God's thoughts on my schedule for that year, and thus I did not know then that God had plans for me to write that book.

There I was, fighting my way through the swamps. I can't tell you how often I wished I had made other decisions for the summer. Usually when a hike or bike ride gets hard, I'm stubborn enough that I double-down on effort and determine I'm going to finish. But the swamps took a toll on my mind and body, and all I could think about was how miserable and lonely I was.

In some areas, fallen trees barred the way, and I had to pick my way through, over, under, and around them. Beaver dams were other obstacles to either portage around or force the kayak over the top. I became quite adept at building up speed and gliding over the rooftops of beaver homes.

One morning I attempted such a maneuver and flipped the kayak. Phone, camera, and captain were soaked. The water wasn't deep, but the episode was frightening and miserable. I righted my craft and pumped out the water. Fortunately, I did have a waterproof bag that kept my clothes dry.

Those miserable days in the swamps were behind me the night I camped on Star Island. The following day, scared but with the knowledge my kayak could roll with the waves, I managed the four-mile crossing to finally put Cass Lake behind me.

Every time one disaster was averted another one presented itself.

I reached an area where wild rice grew. Yes. Wild rice growing in the Mississippi River. It's actually harvested and sold in stores. I was unable to find a channel through this vast rice paddy.

Again, my many prayers asked for direction. When I spotted an opening between two patches of tall swamp weeds, I maneuvered my kayak through the small gap and came out of the weeds to see a building off in the distance.

After reaching the building, I realized it was a series of vacation rentals. I was about to enter one of the largest lakes in Minnesota, Lake Winnibigoshish. I can't pronounce it, either. That's why locals just call it "Big Winnie."

The lake has over 80 miles of shoreline and is 24 miles across. "Danger!" my guidebook warned. "Don't cross this lake if wind conditions are threatening."

I didn't plan to cross. I wanted to live. I'd had enough of wind and waves.

Instead, my plan was to paddle to the right and find a camping spot, then spend the next few days hugging the shoreline until I reached the opposite side at the point the Mississippi left the lake and went on its way.

However, the wind was blowing so hard it was impossible to paddle to the right. The wind blew me to the left, right up on shore where a number of Mennonite families were camping. Of course, I was invited to a meal, and after hearing of the struggles and near disasters I was encountering on the river, one man suggested that he transport me and my kayak around the lake the following morning.

At this offer, I heard words coming out of my mouth I never thought I'd hear.

"That's okay by me."

I rarely give up. I finish what I start. But I was mentally and emotionally exhausted. I tried to convince myself that I would return at a later date and paddle around this lake so that I could say I'd paddled the *entire* Mississippi, but my brain probably knew what my heart wasn't ready to concede: I would never return.

Several days later, I was again struggling to row against the wind. I was discouraged and ready to quit. But that wasn't possible. I was in Minnesota. With only a kayak and no transportation home. The Plan was that my friend would pick me up in New Orleans after my triumphant finish.

My iPhone, baptized the day I'd overturned my kayak, had been lounging in a bed of dehydrated food for a moisture-removal procedure. I had not used it, assuming it was dead. Suddenly the phone came to life. My brother-in-law was calling from the cousins' bus. They were on the return trip. They'd had an enjoyable time. I could have been with them, but no, I had to paddle the Mississippi River.

"We're at Lake Itasca, the spot where you left for your kayak trip. How's it going for you?" he asked.

I wanted to scream, "Miserable! Get me out of here!"

I lost all desire to continue. My sisters and brothers-in-law were on that bus. Family! They were standing where I had started this misery. So close. I wondered if it was possible our paths might cross. Seeing family became far more important than continuing.

Before I could express my thoughts, the phone went dead. In desperation, I tried texting my sister. "Ask the bus driver where he's headed. Could he pick me up?"

"Are you serious?" came the reply.

"Never in my life more serious. I'm done," I sent back.

Shortly after that texted conversation, I pulled up on shore in Cohasset, Minnesota. My phone rang. It was the bus driver, one of my cousins. "Where are you?" he asked.

"I'm in Cohasset, Minnesota."

He looked at his map and announced that they were headed for Cohasset! In an hour or so, their planned route would bring them right through this town.

Amazing! *Thank you, Jesus.*

I was soon reunited with my family. A man in town bought my kayak and equipment. He told me that my choice of kayak was probably what had saved me on Cass Lake. I had bought the sea kayak by choice, but in reality, the "chance" purchase I made (ignorantly, too) was God looking out for me.

I boarded that bus and headed home, realizing that Jesus was already looking out for me the day I purchased the kayak in Chicago. I wouldn't have needed to worry during the lake crossing; Jesus already had met my needs. Jesus also had already established a plan for my extrication from the Mississippi. From beginning to end, He had His eye on me and was taking care of matters when I wasn't even aware of what was happening.

It reminds me of Psalm 139 that says God goes ahead of us and behind us. We're often amazed in looking back and seeing how Jesus has taken care of us, even when we weren't aware we needed Him. And yet, in those in-between times, we sometimes wonder where Jesus is. I know, I've questioned.

Are you currently caught in the middle of a life storm?

Jesus was there before the storm hit, He will be there after it's over, and even if the storm is blinding you and you can't recognize Him, He is right there with you.

He is saying to you, "Take courage! I'm here. Don't be afraid."

22

Storms

It's so relaxing and pleasurable when the seas of life are calm and the sun is shining. The kids are doing well in school. Your spouse is happy to see you. The dog meets you at the front door, tail wagging, happy the master is at home.

Life is much like the children's song we used to sing: "Merrily we roll along, o'er the deep blue sea." There's no sign of turbulence.

But then a little cloud forms on the horizon. Perhaps we should acknowledge it and take precautionary measures. Perhaps we should pull over to the shore. But so often we don't. And suddenly, our little boat is tossing in rough waves under a dark, stormy sky. It may be an emotional or physical storm. It can be devastating news about a loss of some type.

As I prepared to write about the storms we face in life, I received an email containing hurtful words. The words kept me awake most of the night and disrupted my thought process so much I couldn't write one word the following day.

That's the power of spoken words. Words do have meaning. Some words hurt and cut deeply while other words can be a balm for a suffering heart.

Measure your words well. That saying about sticks and stones breaking your bones and words never hurting you is a blatant lie. I would rather be beaten with a stick than have hurtful words spoken to me. A stick hurts the exterior for a while, but hurtful words can do great damage to mind and spirit.

Words spoken to me recently gave me great pain. My boat has been battered and broken during the course of writing this book. However, the storm that churns around and within me is also the reason you're reading this book. Without the devastating blows the storm has delivered, I'd still be in my little boat on a calm sea, enjoying life to the fullest.

All right, perhaps not "to the fullest," but at least pain free.

Is it possible to look back after such a storm and see beauty in the pain? Might I look back in a year and thank God for the turbulence? Are there storms in life that God sends our way to give us a course correction?

I don't know what kinds of seas you are sailing right now. A more important question is whether or not Jesus is in your boat. Perhaps it feels as though He's sleeping like He was one day when the disciples crossed the sea during a storm. It seems He doesn't care what's happening to you, and you are certain you're going to drown. But He is there, and He still has control over all the elements of the storm.

Jesus is watching you in the storm, and perhaps He will come walking to you like He came to the disciples during another storm. His words are still the same to all tempest-tossed disciples: "Don't be afraid. I am here."

You—and I—will weather the storm. Peace! Be still!

23

Sandcastles

As I write, the storm still rages around and within me. My sandcastle has been destroyed, washed out to sea.

These days, I'm feeling something like those men on the road to Emmaus. They carried so much sorrow and had so many questions. Their teacher had been executed, and their dreams, too, had been crushed. Now all kinds of rumors were floating around about the Teacher's body being "missing." Then Jesus joined them on the road; and as they walked along, He gave them new insight into the Scriptures and their hearts "burned" with the hope and truth of God's *living* Word.

As Jesus walks with me through the storm, the Spirit is opening my eyes. Scriptures I've known since a child carry even more meaning for me now. One such passage is the story about two builders, one who builds on rock and one who builds on sand.

Huge crowds were coming to see Jesus. News had quickly spread about His healing power. People traveled from all around the Galilee area to bring their sick and hear Jesus teach. Many came from Jerusalem, about seventy miles away.

Others came from across the Sea of Galilee, from the ten cities making up the Decapolis.

A large crowd had gathered and Jesus went up a mountainside and began to teach them. Matthew 5 gives us His teaching on what we call the Beatitudes. The sermon then continues for three chapters as Jesus teaches on many different topics. If you ever desire to know what "following Jesus" means, these chapters will help you understand.

The final topic from the Sermon on the Mount used builders as an illustration. Jesus said there are wise builders and there are foolish builders. I've been both.

A wise builder, Jesus told the crowd, is anyone who puts into practice what they had just heard. He had supplied the crowd with all the proper materials to build and live in a godly environment. That was a solid foundation on which to build.

It all starts with your foundation. Choose your location wisely. Build your house on rock. Rains will pummel it. Streams will rise and wash against it. The wind will howl and beat against your house. But your house will hold tightly to that solid rock.

I certainly know the difference between rock and sand. However, love wears tinted glasses that can make sand seem like rock, and I was convinced my relationship was built on solid rock.

Make sure you build your future on solid rock. Those of you who are married, hold tightly to Jesus. Never let the devil get even the tiniest foothold in your life. The devil thrives on destroying marriages and relationships.

Emotions can be devastating. We all want to be loved. We all want to feel like we have worth. But building on emotions is building on sand. Jesus is the only person who will truly never leave you or forsake you. Hold tight to the rock that is Jesus and build your relationship on Him.

Have you built a sandcastle that was destroyed? Have you felt the horrible loneliness and helplessness as your dreams are washed away and you can do nothing but watch them go? If you, like me, have had that happen, get on your knees and thank Jesus for the storm.

The pain you're going through is real. But know that Jesus' love lasts. Build on your relationship with Him. Seek higher ground and build on solid rock.

Sandcastles are fun to build. They're just not a good place to dwell if you want to live life. Build and dwell on higher ground.

And don't wait too long!

24

Sowing and Reaping

We have all heard of the law of sowing and reaping. This principle is infallible in our lives: Do not be misled. You can't dishonor God and expect to get away with it. So says Galatians 6:7, in my paraphrase.

A man reaps the same crop that he sows. Oh no, ladies, you're not off the hook here. You also will harvest whatever crop you sow.

I've always known about the principle of sowing and reaping. I've known it since I was a lad, learning from my parents' and my church's teaching—and from my own experience. If I sowed disobedience to my dad, I reaped a spanking. When I was older and could drive, I occasionally drove too fast, and reaped a speeding ticket. In many instances, I knew I was sowing less than good seeds, and I knew I would see the consequences. I never had any doubt that bad sowing would bring a less than desirable harvest.

I always assumed, though, that if I sowed a bad seed, one bad little plant would crop up, a single stalk that could easily be plucked and discarded. Perhaps even a bit of spiritual weed killer could be applied to my undesirable crop, and there! I've taken care of that.

I was so mistaken. I severely miscalculated the harvest.

Harvest time arrived for me when my lady friend found a man she deemed better suited for her. I lost a relationship I trusted and believed in. Shock and devastation filled my soul. *Why, God? Why? We both believed You had brought us together for a purpose.*

I was harvesting vast fields of pain, fields I unknowingly planted with my selfishness. The horrible pain of rejection forced me to survey the pain I myself had sown in others' lives. An apology tour was required. I felt deeply the hurts my selfishness had caused; and, as I asked forgiveness of the folks I had hurt, my tears were from my heart.

Selfishness destroys relationships. Selfishness makes everything about us; our needs come first. I believe selfishness is the root cause of most divorces.

Is your marriage or relationship in trouble? Is selfishness the issue? Examine yourself. Ask God to remove that relationship destroyer from your life. Go back to a pure and true love. Humble yourself before God, and He will give you a heart cleansed from selfishness.

Love is so precious. That feeling of being loved is like no other. A godly marriage or relationship is the closest one can get to Heaven here on earth. If you have that, don't lose it! Fight for it, if necessary. There are so many reasons to fight for love, but one reason can destroy it—selfishness.

Don't ever think you'll reap *only* what you sow. If you sow an acre of pain, seventy acres of harvest will await. If I had to pay real estate taxes on the fields of pain I had to harvest, I'd be broke.

80 DON'T WAIT **TOO LONG**

Sow good seeds. Reap a good harvest. And this law of increased harvest will bless you many times over.

Do you need to ask forgiveness for any selfish acts committed? Don't wait too long.

25

Deception

It should have been Abraham, Isaac, and Esau. Instead, it's Abraham, Isaac, and Jacob.

What happened to the original plan? Deception intervened.

Deception is an evil, destructive tool of selfishness. It causes pain and destroys marriages, relationships, and friendships. You may think you'll get away with your deception, but the law of sowing and reaping applies here as well: He who sows deception reaps deception. The deceiver will be the deceived.

Let's look at a classic example of that in Genesis—the tangled story of Jacob.

Jacob first deceived Esau and his father in order to receive the blessing meant for the first-born. Esau, rightful heir to the blessing, was furious and determined to kill Jacob. Isn't that the first emotion that springs up within when a friend or loved one deceives us? We want revenge! We immediately want to "get even."

Deception severed the relationship between two brothers—twins, as close a bond as brothers could have. The rest of the family was also drawn into the web of deceit. The boys' mother, who was Jacob's co-conspirator in the scheme, warned her favorite son about Esau's planned revenge. She advised Jake to escape to his Uncle Laban's community and stay there until the fire of Esau's anger had cooled.

Misleading, lying, plotting, deviousness—however simple or elaborate, deception becomes a lifestyle for those who practice it. Their guiding principle is *What's good for me?* instead of *What is right and honorable?*

A person who deceives won't be willing to admit they have done so. They often will not even see what they've done as deception. To them, their actions are not wrong. If you try to address the problem with them, they will probably run away (as Jacob did) and will avoid facing you.

But don't plan to kill them. That's frowned upon.

Jacob's story is saturated with deception. When the seeds of deception are planted, the harvest eventually comes. Jacob would soon be reaping what he had sown. The deceiver was about to be deceived.

He arrived at a well near his uncle's place and met some shepherds there. He inquired if they knew his Uncle Laban.

"Yes, we know who Laban is. As a matter of fact, there comes his daughter Rachel now with her father's sheep."

Jacob rolled the stone away from the well and watered his uncle's sheep. He introduced himself to Rachel and kissed her. What? It was probably a customary kiss, perhaps traditional. (I had six dates with my wife before I kissed her the first time. You go, Jacob!) He was welcomed by his relatives, and fell in love with Rachel.

Jacob donated one month of labor to his uncle before approaching him with a deal. He offered to work seven years in exchange for Rachel's hand in marriage. Love is grand. Those seven years possibly felt like mere days to Jacob.

Wedding bells were ringing. Good times were had by all. But Jacob woke up the next morning to find he'd been tricked. Deceived. His new wife was not Rachel but her older sister, Leah. The account in Genesis 29 tells us that Leah had "weak eyes." Some translations say there was no sparkle in her eyes. We can assume she was not very attractive; apparently, the only way she was going to get a husband was through trickery. "But Rachel had a lovely figure and was beautiful" (Genesis 29:17). What had happened to Jacob's eyes? Couldn't he see the woman Laban gave to him in marriage? Perhaps too many wedding toasts were consumed?

Whatever the case, he was deceived. He was reaping what he had sown. See how that works? If you're the one who's been hurt by deceit, you don't have to plot revenge. Deceivers bring it on themselves.

Another deal was made. Jacob agreed to work another seven years for Rachel. But his father-in-law made him a seemingly good offer: Pretend to be Leah's husband for one week, and you can have Rachel, too. What a recipe for disaster.

Deception invaded Jacob's household. Leah tried desperately to win Jacob's love. She thought if she started producing children, she would be a beloved wife. The only result was more children. This put Rachel in a jealous state because she could not get pregnant. She went to Jacob in distress. "Give me children, or I'll die!"

More deception. Rachel gave her maidservant to Jacob to produce children for her gratification. Leah was no longer having children, so she brought her servant Zilpah into the competition to produce more babies. Four women. Thirteen children. Poor Jacob probably couldn't wait to get out of that household every morning.

The seeds Jacob planted when he lied to his father and tricked his brother affected so many people. The harvest continued into the next generation, when eleven boys from three of these women grew up hating the one son that Rachel eventually bore. Joseph, that favored son, ended up thrown into a pit, then sold off to slave traders—by his brothers!

The time came when Jacob had worked long enough for Laban, and he was thinking about going back home. He hoped that Esau had calmed down. But Laban wasn't quite ready to lose Jacob's help.

"How can I convince you to stay?" asked Laban. "Name your price."

I imagine that Jacob's deceptive nature began calculating. Was he still thinking of taking revenge on the man who had deceived him? Or was his scheme merely one more time when he thought, *What's the best plan for me?*

The tangled web of deceit!

Jacob had greatly increased Laban's sheep and goat enterprise but had not built up equity for himself. Another deal was made. Jacob was to receive certain sheep and goats from Laban's flock to build up his own herds. Both Laban and Jacob attempted to cheat the other. Laban contrived to "put a three-day journey between himself and Jacob" (Genesis 30:36) so his scheming would not be detected. Jacob, who had been managing the flock all along, manipulated the breeding of the flock so that he ended up with the strong, healthy stock and Laban was left with the weakest.

Jacob became very wealthy. Naturally, his uncle's attitude toward him changed. So he plotted another deception. He would repeat his previous plan to escape consequences—he'd leave the country. He gathered his huge family, his possessions, and his flocks and left for home. But he wasn't too sure about the reception he would get. Would Esau still be intent on revenge? Jake was rightfully nervous.

He sent messengers ahead to tell Esau he was headed home. They came back with the news that Esau was coming to meet him—along with 400 men.

Now Jacob was shaking in his boots. However, he could still scheme. He split his people and possessions into two groups. If Esau attacked one group, the other would hopefully escape and survive. Jacob also sent large herds of animals ahead as gifts to Esau, hoping this would pacify his brother.

At the stream Jabbok, Jacob sent his entire family and possessions across the ford and headed them toward potential disaster. He alone remained behind.

That night, a wrestling match commenced. The Bible says Jacob wrestled a man all night. Some say it was an angel, but we know that Jacob named the place "Peniel" because it meant he had seen the face of God and survived.

We do know this was a Godly encounter. If it was God, He could have easily overpowered Jacob. But Jacob persisted all night.

Have you ever wrestled with God? Have you persisted all night? I have. I think Jacob wrestling all night is akin to us praying intentionally and persistently about our hurts and desires. We have prayer wrestling matches. That's what I did after the painful breakup.

I lay awake for hours every night. Finally, in my frustration one night, I yelled out to God, "Send me an angel to wrestle!" (I had recently read Jacob's story.)

No angel arrived. Perhaps that was because I was on my back in bed, and it wouldn't have been a fair fight.

I moved my sad self to the living room. It was 2:00 AM. "Come fight with me, God, or send an angel!"

Still nothing. Or was there?

Yes, there was a fight.

I fought the devil as he taunted me with all those thoughts about not being lovable, having no worth, being rejected and deceived.

At daybreak, Jacob's opponent asked to be let go. Since he had not defeated Jacob, he touched his hip and wrenched it out of joint, causing a permanent limp.

The man asked Jacob a question. "What is your name?"

On the surface, it seems like an innocent question. However, the answer tells us that Jacob had turned to speaking truth. "My name is Jacob," he said. Many deceits ago, he had lied to his father and said, "I am Esau, your firstborn."

Truth is the antidote to deceit. Deceit is darkness; truth is light.

The man was a new, redeemed Jacob. When he saw Esau coming toward him with his 400 men, he did not (for once) run away. He did the honorable thing. He went on ahead of his family and met his brother.

Their meeting is a beautiful picture of forgiveness. Esau rushed toward Jacob and wrapped his arms around his brother and kissed him. And then they wept. True forgiveness brings tears of relief.

Have you ever needed to shed tears as you asked forgiveness for your deception? I have. I wept because I had deceived someone myself. I've also been the one who has been hurt and has to forgive deception.

Deception is insidious. Its tentacles can reach into future generations, and unless it is halted and forgiven, it weaves a web that ensnares others. Hebrews 3:13 tells us to encourage others daily so we aren't hardened by sin's deceitfulness. Sin is deceitful. Deceit is sin. Jesus is the answer to that sin.

I don't know where you fit in this story of deceit and its harvest. Have you hurt someone you love? Have you lost a friendship or a relationship because of deceit? Have you been Satan's accomplice in spinning a web of deceit? Jesus can break deceit's webs. Run to Him and ask for His help—quickly, before the web is cast even wider. Ask forgiveness of the person you've hurt. Ask God to give you a new spirit of truth.

Or, have you been deceived and need to forgive but can't? Are you tired, battered, and bruised from battling the emotional effects of deceit? Limp to the one who knows how it feels to be rejected. He will run toward you, embrace you, and hold you in His arms and comfort you. Jesus is the only person who will never leave you or deceive you.

Do it now. Don't wait.

26

Dilemma

As of this writing, I am in a predicament. I have to make a seemingly impossible choice. None of the options available are satisfactory.

My dilemma? Whether or not to forgive. Whether or not it's even *possible* to forgive.

Forgiveness is a basic tenet of Christianity. I've been taught that all my life.

But I have been devastated. Trust was broken. My spirit was crushed. How do I forgive that? My question is this: Do I wait until I'm healed so that I'm able to forgive, or do I forgive so I can heal?

Trying to untangle my thoughts, I called my friend, the prayer warrior.

"You have to forgive her so you can heal. Forgiveness is not about her or what she did to you."

"I can easily forgive when someone comes in sincerity and asks for forgiveness. But just to say, 'Sorry I hurt you' isn't really asking forgiveness."

"She doesn't know that you're still hurting so badly. She doesn't even know she needs to be forgiven. You have to want to forgive. It's a choice you'll have to make."

"Maybe I *don't* want to forgive. Not just yet. I know I need to, and perhaps even want to, but I just can't... yet."

When I'm thinking deeply and trying to pull brilliant lines or desperately needed answers from my brain, I pace. Outdoors, I pace in circles. Indoors, I wear a path on my living room carpet while I ponder. I was pacing during this phone conversation on forgiveness; and at one point, I looked at my Fitbit and realized I had walked 3,000 steps as I talked with my friend.

I'd walked 3,000 steps toward forgiveness. *Dear God, how many steps will it take to get me to real forgiveness?*

Some readers might wonder why I'm being so open and transparent about my struggles with forgiveness in this situation, especially when I claim to be quick to forgive a sincere request for forgiveness.

I'm speaking openly because I believe I speak for many people who feel or have felt the same way. The truth is, it's hard to forgive. It's hard to give the hurt to God and ask Him to deal with it. Those sneaky little longings for revenge or some kind of *justice* are still alive, deep down within, even though everything I've been taught and all that I say I believe is that I must forgive.

I'm also speaking to women who think we men are so strong that we can handle any emotional loss. We can't. We are often pretenders. We men value love, we value honesty, we value truth. We can appear confident on the outside, but we have tender hearts within that can easily be destroyed.

I repeat my dilemma. Does the spirit need to be rebuilt to be able to forgive, or must I forgive so my spirit can be made whole? Does a broken heart have to be mended before it can forgive, or does that heart have to forgive so it can be mended?

Today, the last verse of "Amazing Grace" really spoke to me.

> When we've been there ten thousand years,
> Bright shining as the sun,
> We've no less days to sing God's praise
> Than when we've first begun.
> (John Newton, 1779)

This life is about *the next life.* It's why we have to forgive. It's the price of admission to the eternity we seek. I was reminded of Jesus' words in Mark 11:26: "But if you do not forgive, neither will your Father who is in heaven forgive your transgressions."

I have been forgiven so much.

Dear God, I want to forgive, and I know I need to forgive.

Three thousand steps and counting toward forgiveness.

God, help me not to wait too long.

27

The Cost of Unforgiveness

Whenever I had a chance on my Appalachian Trail hike, I relayed the message I was carrying: Don't take your spouses and families for granted. It's so easy to do when you're swept along by that rushing current of life and living.

During one conversation with a fellow hiker about death and regrets, I told him about the gift of forgiveness I'd been given.

Mary was in the hospital, in the latter stages of her cancer battle. I had already said goodnight and left her room. I remember carrying a stack of books in my hands and walking outside into a light rain. I hunched my shoulders against the drizzle and started for the parking garage.

Then a voice inside me told me to return to Mary's room.

Her room was darkened, and she was sleeping. Sadness swept through me as I looked at her lying there with IV tubes stretched across her body. I went silently to the bedside and touched her shoulder. She was startled awake.

"Paul, what are you doing here? I thought you had gone."

"I was almost to the parking lot when a voice said to come back up here."

"Who told you that?"

"Maybe God. Or just common sense. Or my conscience." (Now, I know it was my Guide pushing me back to that room.) "I need to apologize for not always being the husband I should have been. Too often, I thought of myself first, before you and the family. I'm here to ask forgiveness for my shortcomings as your husband. Will you forgive me?"

Mary forgave me, and we repeated our love for each other. Knowing I had her forgiveness helped me so much as I struggled through the grieving process after her death.

My hiker friend had tears in his eyes as I finished my story. He had lost his dad fifty years before. "I regret so much that I can't ask my dad for forgiveness," he said. "I was a teenager. My dad and I had an argument, and I screamed and cursed at him, then jumped in my car and roared away. While I was gone, my dad died of a heart attack."

This man still felt the devastation of that night, as he recalled those angry words he had hurled at his dad—the last words spoken between them. "That was fifty years ago, and not a day goes by that I don't have regrets about my actions that evening."

"Your dad has forgiven you," I said.

"How would you know that?" he asked.

"Because that's what dads do for their sons," I told him.

My hiker friend had been paying the price of unforgiveness for fifty years. That's a steep price for anyone to pay. I stepped in for his dad and pronounced forgiveness from father to son. The debt was way past due, and now it was canceled.

That's what Jesus did for us. We had a debt so large, a note so big, that only a death could cancel it. Jesus died and marked our note "Paid in Full."

Do you have such a debt on your account that needs to be canceled? Go clear your conscience. Ask forgiveness. A cleansed conscience feels so amazing. I know.

Do it now, while there's still time.

28

5,000 Steps in the Wilderness

I was still reeling days after receiving an email containing what I perceived as hurtful words from the lady I had loved. I called my prayer-warrior friend. I had walked 3,000 steps toward forgiveness during a previous prayer and counseling session, but once again, my mind was in a turmoil.

"Why would she do that?" I lamented, relating how the words in the email had hurt me. "She was so kind to me during the time we were together."

"She really has no idea she hurt you."

"It's so unjust that she's happy and I'm so miserable." In the middle of my lamentations, a thought came to me—several in fact. (I now know it was the Holy Spirit, my Comforter, at work.) One thought was that I was spending too much time looking back. A double-minded man is unstable in all his ways, James wrote. Granted, "unstable" described me and my current condition.

I also realized I was in a wilderness, and I was acting just like the children of Israel as they wandered through the wilderness. They were tired of eating manna, that God-given sustenance that arrived every day. They remembered the fish they had eaten in Egypt. They longed for the cucumbers, melons, leeks, onions, and garlic. They wanted what they thought they had lost rather than the food God was providing. I was tired of eating manna, too. God was leading me to a promised land, a land of plenty. Through this wilderness, He was providing for each day, but I was looking back at what I thought I had lost rather than focusing on the promised land where God was leading me. I was still looking back to my captivity to kindness.

During this phone conversation, I walked 5,000 steps. Five thousand more steps in the wilderness.

Pass the manna, please.

29

Be Honorable

Being in love is an amazing feeling. To care for someone and have them care for and about you makes life a joy. The Bible is filled with verses about love. The Song of Songs has eight chapters filled with love and passion.

Yet many of us also know the devastation of love gone wrong. I've experienced the pain of rejection, but I've also been the one who has rejected others. Let's broaden our discussion of these truths even further. Many of you have suffered broken relationships of other kinds—divorce, estranged children, friendships that have died, or family members who have been alienated. It's my prayer that even though your situation might be different than mine, the thoughts I share will be of some help to you.

Granted, some relationships *must* be ended for the good of both people. Ending such a relationship is the right thing to do.

However, there is also a right way to conduct ourselves in such a situation. Sow seeds that will give you a good harvest.

Love is patient, love is kind. It does not envy, it does not boast, it is not proud. It does not dishonor others, it is not self-seeking, it is not easily angered, it keeps no records of wrong. (1 Corinthians 13:4-5)

This passage says love "does not dishonor others." That gives me pause. Have you ever felt dishonored in a breakup? I'm sure many of you have. It's more painful than any physical pain. Those of us who have been on the rejected side of a relationship know the pain. Those who have been on the other side have also felt pain in the situation. Pain often propels us to defend and protect ourselves and lash out at others. Pain is fertile ground where selfishness can so easily take root.

But God's Word says love will not dishonor others. "Others" seems to gather everyone under the same umbrella, doesn't it? Whether a person has treated us rightly or wrongly, love still treats them with respect.

If you are the one breaking a relationship, the other person deserves the dignity of answers. They need clarity so healing can begin. To deny them answers and truth is the ultimate in cruelty. Half-truths and partial answers only delay the healing process. I can handle any truth, but lies or deception will devastate me. Yes, a truthful conversation will be painful for both parties, but at least the truth is revealed and healing can begin.

Never begin a new relationship before ending the old one. Dishonor and deception creep in here, too. You'll be sending a message that says, "You're not good enough. I'm looking for someone better." Yes, there might be another person that is a better fit for you, but for the sake of the one you once said you loved, honor them by ending that relationship first.

If you are on the other side of a broken relationship, you, too, must beware of dishonoring the person who has in one way or another brought pain to you. Guard your tongue. Better yet, ask the Spirit to guard your tongue; too often, our "guards" are much too feeble. Guard your ears, too—be careful what you listen to. Don't give ear to those who want to gossip or tear down the person who has hurt you. Keep your anger and pain off social media, the fastest way to spread destructive wildfire. And ask God for a cleansing of your own heart and thoughts, so that you truly will be loving and not dishonor that other person.

Let me be clear, relationships can be broken and many times need to be broken. No matter what the situation, a broken relationship is a great loss and it does need to be grieved. But dishonor will inflict even greater wounds—on everyone.

30

Rejection

Rejection at some point in life is inevitable for most of us. A job you were convinced was yours goes to a less-qualified applicant. A relationship that seems perfect turns out to be a mirage. Someone you trust betrays that trust. A child leaves home in anger and wants no more contact with you. Someone who claimed to love you turns away and slams the door.

Rejection leaves devastation in its wake. For many of us, unless we can understand *why* we've been rejected, we're taken to the edge of insanity. It's that dangerous.

Having wandered in this wilderness for a time, my purpose and prayer now is that I can give some insight to folks who have felt the pain of being told—outright or by implication—that they weren't good enough. Hopefully, the conveyors of such pain might also find insight on how devastating rejection can be to another human being.

Several years ago when I ended a relationship with another lady, I thought I did it in an honorable fashion. I faced her and told her why I believed it was best we separated. But I had no concept of what that rejection did to her spirit. That is, I didn't understand until it happened to me. That law of sowing and reaping keeps cropping up in my life.

Then, when the lady I had recently loved and honored for two years met someone she felt was a "better fit" for her lifestyle, my spirit was shattered. I was devastated. I had been rejected.

How does one recover? That's been my question. I tried a number of ways, some of them right, some wrong.

My initial reaction was the wrong way. I believed she had treated me in a dishonorable way and I deserved answers. I went about seeking answers. I needed to know what I had done that changed her mind about our love. My mind couldn't grasp what had just happened. However, there were no answers that could possibly satisfy me. But I *had* to have answers.

I couldn't eat; I couldn't sleep. My weight dropped precipitously. I continued to push for answers, but I only managed to anger and frustrate her.

How could I have better handled this rejection? Perhaps you can learn from my mistakes.

Finally, after burning all my bridges and losing every possible form of communication with this person, I did a few things right. Here's free advice, should you ever find yourself on the receiving end of rejection or deception. (Well, perhaps it's not entirely free if you purchased this book.)

If you're in a relationship and your love isn't enough to keep your partner from looking elsewhere for better options, you also don't have enough love to win him or her back.

Know that the person who has devastated your life can't possibly fix your heart. They neither can nor want to. They have moved on. They cannot know the horrible feelings and thoughts that have attacked you.

If you've been rejected, self-worth drops as low as zero, perhaps even lower. It's important to have a support group or at least several friends with soft shoulders to cry on. Discuss your feelings of rejection with your friends. Chances are good that they have experienced something similar in their lives and can relate. It often feels as though you're going through this wilderness solo. Knowing friends have survived rejection in some form might give you hope for your own recovery. Honest friends are a godsend. I tended to look back and lament what I thought I had lost. My friends helped me see what parts of those memories were merely a mirage.

After a romantic failure, life may seem to hold no meaning. However, push yourself to put life in perspective. Instead of focusing solely on your pain, try to see the big picture of your life. Surely there are other meaningful aspects besides that one lost love. Find distractions. Go for walks. Recall what brought you joy before you fell in love and return to those things.

Journal. But a word of warning. That journal is for you and the healing of your wounded heart. I spilled many words over my keyboard. I sent it to my former friend, thinking she should know how much she had hurt me. *Bad idea.*

What followed all my bad ideas was the deepest period of grieving in my life. Yes, I grieved the death of my wife deeply. She passed away and went to Heaven. With her went life as I had known it, all our shared memories, and our plans for the future. But we had not lost our love for each other. This recent grieving was for shattered love, devastated self-worth, destroyed trust, and, again, loss of dreams.

The deep grief led me to my best idea: I took the pieces of my heart and gave them to the one person who could return my heart to peace—Jesus. Much of what you have read here is the outcome of the time I've spent with Him.

In the process, I became aware of the pain I had caused others, and with a broken spirit and tears, I repented and asked God for forgiveness for the hurts I'd caused. Then I went on that apology tour and asked forgiveness of the people I'd hurt.

And finally, acknowledge mistakes you have made in the relationship and determine not to repeat them. Give your love to someone who will return it, and then never take that loved one for granted.

> Above all else, guard your heart, for it is the wellspring of life. (Proverbs 4:23)

The guard is back. He's guarding a dry well. The water of love that flowed so freely has turned to tears that now flow freely. Do tears cleanse one's heart and soul? If so, mine are about to shine brilliantly again.

My prayer is that I find love again. I pray the wellspring of my heart will once more flow freely. That will require trust. It seems elusive now.

But I pray I don't have to wait too long.

31

Rejection Survival Guide

Those on the receiving end of rejection will understand these thoughts:
She broke up with me because I'm not good enough.
He doesn't want me because I'm not worthy.
I don't matter to anyone.
I'm insignificant.
It's not safe to give my trust to anyone.
That's the pattern of thoughts bombarding a person who has been rejected. The thoughts feed feelings of despair, insignificance, loneliness, and yes, anger and vengefulness.

How does one recover? How do we cleanse ourselves of all that swamp muck and think clearly again?

Go to Jesus. He is the one person who will never break your trust. He has the power to cleanse and restore.

Desperate, I went to Him. Recovery was a slow, painful process. But He's led me along the way, and the process still goes on.

Searching the Scriptures for passages to aid my healing, I used my phone to keep images of the verses that spoke to me.

They're still on my phone, and I go back to them often, reading and re-reading His Word. I've already shared some of these throughout this book. Here are a few more, with my brief notes.

> The righteous cry out, and the LORD hears them; He delivers them from all their troubles. The LORD is close to the brokenhearted and saves those who are crushed in spirit. (Psalm 34:17-18)

I spent far too much time thinking about our past. It's so easy to get stuck in memories of the wonderful times that were once ours but are now lost to us. Memories were so painful—but my mind was stuck in the past. I cried out to God for a verse that might help.

> But one thing I do: Forgetting what is behind and straining toward what is ahead, I press on toward the goal to win the prize for which God has called me heavenward in Christ Jesus. (Philippians 3:13)

It's hard to forget what is behind when those times were so beautiful. But I strained and strained... and I became drained and drained. I couldn't sleep; I couldn't eat; I was in a downward spiral.

God, I need a verse to get me through another day. I often turned to my friend David for helpful words.

> Turn to me and be gracious to me, for I am lonely and afflicted. The troubles of my heart have multiplied; free me from my anguish. (Psalm 25:16-17)

The troubles of my heart did multiply as the thoughts swirling through my mind paralyzed me for days on end. *God, I need a verse today. Again.*

> We demolish arguments and every pretension that sets itself up against the knowledge of God, and we take captive every thought to make it obedient to Christ. (2 Corinthians 10:5)

My thoughts stampeded through my mind like wild stallions in the West. They needed to be corralled and broken. It was not possible to do that on my own. I gave them over to God. This capturing and making obedient is a difficult process, but if thoughts are allowed to run freely, they'll consume your mind and energy to the point where happiness and joy cannot return.

As Christians, we have the promise that one day there will be no more suffering. However, in this life we will encounter various types of suffering: ill health, emotional suffering, or persecution for our faith. My heart was broken, but my love for Jesus was strong and I know He will never break my trust. "Trust God," He said. "Trust me." (John 14:1) I'm trusting Him as the healer. He has the power to heal shattered hearts and dreams. God promises restoration for those who cry out to Him. I've cried!

I've written so openly about my experience because I hope there are lessons to be learned for all of us, whether you've gone through a devastating breakup or not. But by far the two most important and effectual tips I can give you are these: Cry out to God. And go to His Word for healing truths.

32

Heart Condition

How's your heart? Is your heart a pathway? A rock? Full of thorns? Or noble and good?

Luke 8 includes the parable of the sower. Even these well-known passages bring us new revelations if our hearts and minds are open to the Spirit's teaching. This is what happened to me one morning as I read Luke 8 and realized how much it tells us about heart conditions.

Jesus was going about His business, traveling from town to town. All twelve disciples were with Him, as were several women. Mary Magdalene was one of the women; Jesus had cast seven demons out of her. Susanna and Joanna, also healed by Jesus, were two more.

Luke tells us the women were contributing "their own resources" to help the ministry. I find it interesting that Joanna was married to a guy named Chuza, and Chuza was the manager of the household of Herod. Now, we can probably assume that Herod paid Chuza, who in turn may have given money or resources to his wife, Joanna, who then helped support Jesus' ministry. We don't know about Chuza's belief or lack of it, but I'm sure Herod would not have approved of this. What a contrast between the heart of Joanna and the cruel Herod!

Jesus started speaking to a large crowd. He spoke about farming and sowing seeds, a picture that would have been very familiar to most of His audience. A farmer in that day may have had only a container from which he dispersed the seeds by hand. Some might possibly have had a type of seed broadcaster. The focus of Jesus' story was not on the scattering of seeds, but on the ground on which the seed fell.

Some seed fell on a nearby path. It was trampled on, and the birds had a free meal.

Some seed fell on rocks and found enough soil to take temporary root—but not enough moisture to sustain life.

Some seeds landed where thorns also grew. The thorns choked out any seedling brave enough to make an appearance.

Finally, fortunate seeds landed on good ground and produced one hundred times what was sown.

"If you have ears that can hear, you should be hearing this," Jesus said, winding up the parable.

Apparently, the disciple's ears weren't attuned enough; they didn't understand what Jesus was saying. My own spiritual "ears" opened a bit more as I read on…

The farmer is Jesus, and the seed is the Word of God. Verse 15 of chapter 8 says the seed that took root and produced a harvest is like the Word taking root in folks with noble and good hearts. The Word is held in those hearts and brings a bountiful harvest.

That verse stopped me. If good ground where seeds can take root represents a good heart, what are the heart conditions portrayed in the other three examples? I needed to go back a few verses, read again, and reflect on my own heart condition.

A thorny heart does hear but is so distracted by worry, the desire to get rich, and the chase of pleasure that the Word is choked out. There's no place for the seed to grow, and the thorns remain and overrun the ground.

The rocky heart receives the seed gladly and does a few hallelujahs and praise-the-Lords but quickly closes shop when it is tested.

The pathway heart steps on the seed. It recognizes the Word, but the devil quickly snatches away any seeds before they can take root and produce fruit.

You have one of those four heart conditions. Are you a pathway heart, a rocky heart, a thorny heart, or a good and noble heart?

Do you need a new heart? Are you a bit like the Tin Man in the Wizard of Oz, rusting away in the forest and wishing for a heart? If so, you have a choice. There are four types of hearts available.

The Sower is scattering the seed right now. Which heart will the Seed find in you?

33

Double-Minded Hearts

For obvious reasons, in the last few months I've spent an unusual amount of time thinking about our hearts and minds, our thoughts and our emotions. Many verses in the Bible focus on these forces within that shape our actions and our lives. Those thoughts that need to be captured. The hearts that are broken. The hearts full of deceit. Spirits that are crushed. The heart that loves by action. The mind focused on the goal and the prize. The truths are spelled out for us in God's Word, and we do well to learn from them. I found my own heart, mind, and spirit described in many passages.

I realized, for example, that I was a double-minded man—because of my double-minded heart. If that sounds a bit unstable... well, it is.

If you've ever been caught in a rip current, you know how quickly fear can well up within you. But in a rip current, fear can kill you. It is possible to survive such a current; and if you know what to do and have faith in that knowledge, it can save your life. However, there's no room for doubt. If you waver, the rip current will win.

110 DON'T WAIT **TOO LONG**

James 1:6-8 speaks of the person who is double-minded, one who says he has faith but also entertains fears and doubts. That man is unstable, tossed about like a wave of the sea driven by the wind. That is what happens when we allow our minds to go unchecked. We imagine the worst, we conjecture, we strain to figure out the unexplainable. If those thoughts aren't taken captive, they lead to an unstable life. That is what the devil wants.

A double-minded person might also be one who keeps looking back to the past. Most of us may at times recall some event or relationship in the past and feel regret. But do you dwell on those regrets? Or have you been hurt deeply and now can't control those endless, roiling thoughts that keep stirring up the mud and dirtying the water of your mind? Those thoughts focused on the past seem to control your very being and keep you from living today and going forward. Thoughts are just thoughts; they aren't reality. Yet one's imagination about past events can stifle forward progress.

Your head and your heart are trying to live in two different places. You're caught between fear and faith; or you can't move forward because your heart and mind are stuck in the past. You are double minded.

Both fear and the shadows of the past can keep you from committing completely to the task at hand. That task is following Jesus wherever He will take you; everything else must take second priority. But as long as your mind is looking in two directions, you are unstable.

James wrote that the double-minded and unstable person should not expect to receive anything from the Lord (James 1:7). That's a strong warning, my friend!

Whatever rip current you're caught in right now, keep your eyes on the Champion, Jesus. Don't allow fear or pain to overpower your faith. Don't allow the past to deny the present and the future. Allow Jesus to speak peace to the storm and to take those troublesome thoughts captive.

34

Plowed Heart

Our hearts can also be compared to fields that must be plowed. They will be plowed, no doubt about it.

I've had a painful gouge plowed across my heart. The plow of despair broke me open and inflicted a wound so devastating I had no place to go but to God. I couldn't eat, I couldn't sleep. I cried out for healing and begged God for peace.

However, something amazing started to happen. Something miraculous. Out of my wounded heart, the selfish acts of my past that had hindered me in my Jesus-walk poured out. With that cleansing, my heart became fertile ground, allowing good seed to be sown in the open furrows.

The wound remained, but the furrow closed and the seed rested in the tomb of my heart, awaiting death and transformation. Yes, those seeds planted in my broken heart had to die so new life could begin.

In this in-between time, we wait. And the heart changes—a tomb of death becomes a womb holding the seeds of new life.

Then the miracle of new birth happens. A little stem protrudes where the scar of pain still exists. Light and water give it encouragement. It comes from darkness to light, from death to life. A new crop emerges, with seventy, even one hundred, times what was planted.

Soon it will be time to reap what has been sown. A harvest awaits.

Good seed planted in this in-between time will produce a good harvest. Choose wisely what you plant.

35

The Stained-Glass Heart

It's been a long in-between time for me. For months, I was consumed by feelings of rejection and loneliness. Yes, consumed. Those feelings ate me up. Devoured me.

One day on my walk with God, I again recited my lament of lost love. The thoughts that ate holes in me were always along these lines: *You weren't good enough for her. She found someone else while still with you. You weren't worthy of her love.*

I needed to concentrate on writing projects, but these thoughts held my brain and heart captive. Other thoughts found no place to settle in, put down roots, and grow into anything productive.

There is a reason Jesus said the Holy Spirit would be our Comforter and our Advocate: He comes to our rescue and aid. That day, He showed me clearly that it was the devil I was meeting in battle. The enemy of my soul was whispering—no, screaming—those awful thoughts, and my broken heart had no resistance to fight off the attack.

"Your heart is like glass that she shattered. Your whole relationship was built out of glass. She didn't care about you at all. There are days she gives you no thought. She's moved on, and you are left in pieces. The broken glass of your heart can never be put back together," shouted the devil.

Yes, it can, replied a soft voice. It was God's turn to talk.

I can put glass back together. When I put broken glass back together, it's a work of art, a stained-glass masterpiece.

I can take those shards and bind them together to make a heart of unimaginable beauty. I am the bonding agent that brings and holds them all together.

The deeper your pain, the deeper will be the hues of your stained-glass heart. And once again, beautiful colors of love will pour out from you.

About that time, the devil slunk away. He knew he'd been caught in his lies.

Someday God will answer my prayer for a godly wife to love, to honor, and to cherish. She will look into my eyes and see my stained-glass heart, with all its love streaming outward, and she'll exclaim, "I have one just like that!"

36

You Are Loved

Have you been rejected or abandoned by someone you loved? If so, you know the feeling of not being valued enough to be held in their lives. That feeling of not being valued is destructive. It's devastating.

But do you know the plan God has for you?

Long ago, God had you in mind. Before He created the world, He knew about you. You were part of His grand plan.

According to Ephesians 1, the plan was that through Jesus we would stand before God, holy and without fault. We would be adopted into God's family as sons and daughters, heirs to everything He has. He was *pleased* to do this! It pleases Him to take you into His family, to give you access to all His resources, and to give you access to Himself, the great Creator.

Those who come to God through Jesus stand before Him covered with love. Can you imagine a love so strong it will overlook all our faults and failures and still love us?

Why would God do that? Because He wanted to.

But why would He want to?

He sees us as gifts. Gifts to Himself. However, to receive us as gifts, He needed someone to present these gifts to Him. That's where Jesus came in. Through Jesus, we now become these precious gifts to God.

God even has a plan to send Jesus back to collect the gifts still here on earth at His chosen time. Won't that be an amazing Christmastime in Heaven—when all those gifts arrive!

Amazing, isn't it? God chose us. We have value.

Know that you have one true friend who will never leave you or reject you. Your friend is Jesus. Accept the gift God gave you of Jesus, so that Jesus in turn can give God the gift that is you.

God chose us. He values us. He loves us.

37

"Come and Dine"

Do you like a good fish story?

Every Thursday, I meet a good friend for lunch. We help each other solve problems, and we two together solve other people's problems. That's usually easier than solving our own. From the outside looking in, solutions often seem obvious. Our own problems, however, seem insurmountable when we're lost in our own head. My friend and I shine sunlight into each other's fog bank.

At a recent lunch, my friend informed me a co-worker wished to speak to me about hiking, and we invited him to join us. He was an upbeat man, genial and kind. He had one less arm than we did, having lost an arm in an industrial accident.

We talked hiking, but then our conversation turned to fishing. At some point, my friend said, "This guy can do anything any other person with two arms can do."

"Oh no, he can't," I interjected. "He can't lie about the size of the fish he caught." We all laughed heartily. Great. The guy had a good sense of humor as well.

That conversation about fishing reminded me of another fish story in the Bible. Fishermen are known to exaggerate in their telling of fish tales. This Biblical account is very precise. These fishermen caught 153. (There must have been no limit back then on the Sea of Galilee.)

But 153 is the end of the story. The beginning of the story is that they had fished all night and come up with nothing.

This encounter took place after Jesus had risen from the dead, but before He had ascended to Heaven. The disciples had returned home, and that night, they were fishing on the Sea of Galilee. The night fishing had been disastrous, but morning was coming.

On the shore, a solitary silhouette appeared. The person was unrecognizable in the predawn light. However, the stranger called out to them with fishing advice.

"Children, did you catch anything?" He shouted.

"Nothing. Not one fish."

"Your net is on the wrong side. Toss it over on the right side, and you'll find fish."

Imagine that. There couldn't have been much space between the left side and the right side. The fish were there; they just needed a fish finder. The man on shore certainly had some credibility as a fish finder—he already had fish cooking over burning coals.

The fishermen took the advice and caught so many fish they couldn't even haul the net into the boat. Can't you see them rowing into shore, dragging that net full of fish?

That is, all but one disciple were rowing.

Simon Peter had finally recognized who was on the shore and tried out his recently learned skill of water walking. They were three hundred feet offshore when he jumped into the water and splashed toward the beach.

The boat followed, dragging the net full of fish. These weren't small fish; they were large fish. A grand total of 153 large fish. More fish than the new net could have held without tearing.

I like the King James version of what came next—an invitation from the Master to a meal.

"Come and dine."

Whenever I hear that phrase, I become very nostalgic, recalling my dad's voice. From our porch every evening at five o'clock, the cry went out to join the master at the table.

There were seven of us: Mom and Dad and five children. We five children could be scattered all around the property, perhaps playing croquet, perhaps taking turns riding the old rusty bicycle someone had gifted us. Dad couldn't afford a bicycle, so an uncle had given us an old used one. We didn't have a lot of money, but we made up for that in love. So much love. So many precious memories.

Dad would call us "chilllens." He'd come out to the front porch every evening and call, "Chillens, come and dine!" Wherever we were on the old homestead, we heeded that call. We joined the master at the supper table and we prayed. Then we dined. Then we prayed again. Prayer was vital in our master's house.

Are you frustrated that nothing ever seems to work out for you? Has it been a long, unsuccessful night in the in-between valley? Are you casting your net on the wrong side of the boat?

Try a different approach. Cast your net in a different direction. The difference between faith and fear is a new direction. The difference between eternal life and eternal death is a new direction.

Direct your eyes and ears to the man on shore. He cries out to you, "Come and dine." Sit down with the Master. Come as you are. It's a carry-in. Whatever you're carrying, bring it in. Don't wait too long. Get to know him.

Your long night of difficulties, sadness, and pain is about to end. The dawn of change has arrived.

Will you accept this invitation?

>Jesus has a table spread
>Where the saints of God are fed,
>He invites His chosen people, "Come and dine;"
>With His manna He doth feed
>And supplies our every need:
>Oh 'tis sweet to sup with Jesus all the time!
>
>"Come and dine," the Master calleth, "Come and dine;"
>You may feast at Jesus' table all the time,
>He who fed the multitude, turned the water into wine,
>To the hungry calleth now, "Come and dine."
>   (Charles B. Widmeyer, 1906)

38

Monarchs

People collect the oddest things. I used to collect matchbooks. Later, I amassed a wealth of pens. Every time I've played a round of golf, I saved the scorecard. (But I'd be embarrassed to display that collection.) Upon my demise, these assembled treasures will be among the first loads of trash my kids carry to a dumpster.

I've also collected some antiques and art objects that, if sold properly, should sustain me for one month in a modest nursing home. If that is never necessary, I certainly hope my kids realize there's more than matchbook value there and exchange these for filthy lucre.

I say all this to show the difference in the collecting styles of the Mrs. and me. I collected some things with zero value and some items that surely will have increased in value over time. My wife collected worms! At least, worms were free.

Okay, *worms* sounds so coarse. Mary collected caterpillars, or larvae. You could also say that she collected hope, because she was looking ahead to the beautiful winged creatures that the worms would someday become.

She drove along country roads, looking for milkweed plants. Monarch butterflies lay their eggs on this plant, and after the eggs hatch, the larvae (the tiny little worms) munch on the leaves relentlessly. From the plant, the caterpillars ingest a type of poison—not harmful to the caterpillar, but quite repugnant to birds looking for a bug feast. God has designed that built-in protection for the tiny creatures.

When Mary found caterpillars, she collected them along with a handful of leaves and deposited all in a quart jar covered with a screen in place of the usual lid. For two weeks after hatching, a caterpillar eats those leaves at a voracious pace. Finally, bursting at the seams with milkweed ingredients, the youngster is ready to sprout wings.

The larva attaches itself to a twig by spinning a bit of silk around itself, wrapping itself tightly in a beautiful green casing called a chrysalis. Then it waits. Not much seems to be happening, but a miracle of change is taking place within. Within two weeks, the chrysalis starts to darken, losing the green color and becoming almost translucent. Patterns of orange and black can be seen within. That worm is undergoing an amazing transformation, changing its method of locomotion from a creepy crawler to a beautiful creature with wings.

The monarch butterfly that emerges is sometimes called "The Wanderer." It flits and floats about, going from flower to flower, having the time of its two-week life. It then lays eggs and dies.

This happens two more times. Then, in the fourth generation, a miracle occurs. The fourth generation of monarch butterflies—emerging from the chrysalis stage in the fall of the year—is born to travel. And travel it does. Instead of the fourteen-day life span of its parents, grandparents, and great-grandparents, this generation will live from six to eight months, joining human snowbirds and heading south for a warmer climate. After wintering in Mexico, some inner knowledge tells Mr. and Mrs. Butterfly it's time to start the journey back home. And the four-generation cycle starts again.

We humans are a bit like worms—uh, that is, caterpillars.

Aren't you tired of being a worm, crawling around on sixteen legs? Don't you wish you could soar?

You can soar spiritually. You can discern the mysteries of the universe—but only if you undergo a metamorphosis yourself. That mysterious miracle of change is what happens when the Holy Spirit births a new life in you. Scriptures tell us He is changing us—a fundamental change from the old person into a new person, from the old me into a person like Christ!

Introspection

As I described in the first paragraphs of this book, I had been enjoying a season of peace. During that time, my thoughts were going frequently to my aloneness, and my prayer was that I would find love again. I asked God for someone with whom I could share life and make memories. Someone who would go with me through both the good times and the bad times as we supported each other. Is it possible to experience the wonderful feeling of love again at my age?

Yes, it is!

You've been reading about how that beautiful miracle of love happened to me. It was a fairy-tale romance. Our fairy tale ended sadly. For me, in devastating fashion.

Somewhere in the last few months, I read a statement that caused me to wonder if it described my situation. This is the statement: The wrong person will find you in peace and leave you in pieces, but the right person will find you in pieces and lead you to peace.

Had I really found the wrong person? I couldn't begin to imagine that. It seemed our love was so strong. Our love was a miracle. We were both convinced that God had brought us together. She was so special and kind. What had gone wrong? Wasn't I a child of God? Wasn't I special too? Wasn't this an answer to my prayers?

It was time for some painful introspection. I've had to do this several times in my life—to take a good, honest look at myself and go behind the curtain where my thoughts and aspirations and intentions lie. It's a place where I often fear to tread myself.

I knew I had built a wall between my mind and my heart. My heart lived on feelings my brain could never grasp. My mind often knew the realities of the relationship, but that wall was solid and prevented any messages from my mind reaching my heart. The base of that wall between mind and heart was littered with thoughts and feelings that had been stopped short in transit.

After the fairy tale ended, I needed answers. I needed to know why she rejected me. Nothing she would or could tell me satisfied my desperate mind. No emails or phone calls could give me peace. Finally, she asked me to stop. Just stop.

I knew I had to take a journey, one that was many years past due. It was a trip to a foreign land, but no passport would be required. Just courage and honesty. I needed to take a journey to the center of my being.

Lao Tzu wrote: "Knowing others is intelligence. Knowing yourself is wisdom." I believed I was wise—I've always prayed for it—and now wisdom demanded that inner journey.

How about you, reader? Are you experiencing any of these things I've been through? Have you been rejected? Or have you treated someone dishonorably? Have you been the deceived or the deceiver? Are you tired and weary of your lot in life? Does it seem as if God is blessing everyone around you—but not you? Are you weary of your trudge through the in-between valley?

If there is any area of your life in pieces instead of in peace, maybe it's time to take a trip. Take the flashlight of truth and honesty with you. Go courageously. Be prepared for pain and possibly even some ugliness. Get ready to forgive someone, perhaps even yourself. You may have to break down some walls on the way in, but do it.

Go with this prayer from Psalm 119, first uttered by my friend David: "Keep me from lying to myself; give me the privilege of knowing your instructions."

40

Darkening Chrysalis

I actually researched introspection. Instructions said, *Find a place where you can be alone with your thoughts. A comfortable place. Perhaps a walk in the woods.*

I knew instinctively where to go.

A year after Mary and I were married, we purchased a piece of land on a hilltop overlooking beautiful Amish farmland. It is a lovely site, and we planned to build a house there and raise our family. In the ensuing years, we often went there to walk and dream about the future.

Sadly, that's all I did—dream.

I delayed, I procrastinated. Children were born; we couldn't move then—that would mean changing school districts. We built other houses elsewhere, building and selling, waiting until the day when at last we could afford to build exactly what we wanted. Reason after reason and excuse after excuse ate away the years.

Thirty years later, my wife left this earth. Our dream home was never built.

In the years since my wife's passing, I often go to that hilltop to walk, reflect on missed opportunity, and dream of future possibilities. The question hangs in the air on that hill: Can I still have that house and a beautiful lady to love?

This was where I must conduct my introspection.

Most fairy tales about love end up with "and they lived happily ever after." And you've heard those fantasies about kissing a frog and a prince appears? My story is this: She kissed a worm, and I remained a worm.

However, a worm has great hope: It has the potential to change.

As I left my house that day, determined to find some answers on why I do or don't do anything, I thought about the current state of my mind and heart. Following the devastating breakup, I had wrapped myself up in pain and despair. What had I done wrong? My mind spun endlessly, trying to make sense of it all, looking for the key to the puzzle. I had no joy in life. No passion for living. Day after day, night after night my mind had spun in circles. I was a worm spinning a chrysalis around me. Like those caterpillars Mary had collected and watched so closely as they spun the casing around themselves, my mind and body became tightly ensconced in thoughts and feelings about loss and rejection.

Yes, my life was like a worm, wrapped up tightly in a chrysalis.

I drove through town on my way to my hilltop that day. A new food truck had joined the many attractions along Main Street—a new coffee vendor. I had already passed the location when I realized what I had read on the sign: The name of the coffee bar was Chrysalis coffee.

Was that just a coincidence? God wouldn't direct that coffee bar to arrive there on that day to send me a message—

or would He? However, He had reminded me that I was indeed a worm in a chrysalis with the potential to become a butterfly.

I cried all the way to the hilltop.

On the crest of the hill, I took in the beauty surrounding my parcel of land. I let my mind drift to the past, so many years ago, when the dream was in its infancy. So many *what ifs* roiled my thoughts and feelings. And always, the more recent memories pushed their way to the forefront. Those memories were what had brought me here to dreamland.

Long ago, I had love. Sadly, I often took it for granted. Now I had been blessed with another lady to love and had vacillated once again. Why do I do that?

I crept into the inner chambers of self to see what could be discovered.

Wow, it's dark in here. Where's that flashlight of truth?

I'm your conscience. I'll be your guide today. Follow me. I'll ask you a few questions and you must answer honestly.

Agreed. I love truth.

What do you like about life?

Right now, nothing. In the recent past, I loved flowers, music, and travel.

Why not now?

They all remind me of time spent with my lady friend. Those memories cause such pain. I'm tired of pain.

Whose fault is it that you are experiencing such pain?

Well… hers, of course!

Are you sure?

I certainly wouldn't bring that on myself, would I?

Perhaps you did. Let's explore further. What do you desire most in life?

Besides my desire to follow and honor Jesus, it's being in love. I want to love and be loved.

So, you had that and now don't?

My siblings and children and grandchildren love me, but to be complete, I also need the love of a godly woman.

What else do you desire from life?

When I was in my twenties, I desired wealth. I worked hard toward that goal but never became wealthy. We were debt free and had enough to live comfortably, but not much more than that.

Lao Tzu, who you quoted previously, said that if you realize you have enough, you are truly rich.

I suppose that makes me rich then.

What do you want from a relationship?

I desire love, honesty, and honor.

The thing you desire most is truth. I am truth. Rethink your entire love story from beginning to end. See who really failed. Go back even further. Go back to when you first loved and lost. Start there. When did you get the first taste of rejection?

Oh that? How brutal! I was sixteen and in love with a beautiful girl. I believed she was my future. However, she fell in love with another, and the rejection broke my heart. It took a year to overcome that loss. Of course, she never knew or realized what she had done to my spirit. I hate rejection!

Why?

Why? Because it makes me feel worthless. It makes me think I'm not worthy of anyone's love.

Why were you rejected?

I don't know.

You do know. Go back again in time. Not to your first love. Go to your second love.

Oh, yes, Mary. Yes, I messed that up, didn't I? We dated for a few years, and foolish me couldn't make up my mind about marriage. I broke up with her. I thought perhaps I needed to date other girls. I thought maybe there was a better choice out there.

And what happened?

It only took a day or two to realize how lonely I was and how much I missed her. Fortunately, she still loved me enough to take me back, and I realized I already had the best choice. But by my foolishness and procrastination, I nearly missed out on her love. I almost waited too long.

That's it! There's my answer! I wait too long in relationships.

I have no problems making decisions about any other endeavors in life. I actually consider myself a risk taker. I'm willing to take big risks for big rewards. Quitting my job and hiking the Appalachian Trail was one of my biggest risks. A chain of events after that hike brought this lady to me. Our connection was from God, we both thought. How could such a beautiful beginning end so badly?

Part of that answer lies right where you are standing. On your hilltop dream land.

I got it. I saw the entire puzzle, piece fitting into piece. The first time my new love had come to visit me, I had brought her to this very hill. I explained how much this site meant to me and talked about my dream of a house here someday. She had loved the view and also fell in love with the idea of a home there. As we fell deeper in love, she mentioned the house on the hill a few times. We had discussed living in Amish Country a few months a year and living a few months a year in her hometown. In addition, she wanted to purchase a house on a beach in Florida, to spend our winters there.

Recapping the facts was painful. We loved each other. She was kind. She was beautiful. She loved God. She was everything I had ever prayed for. God gave me all that, and yet here I was alone on my dream hilltop.

Why? I waited too long.

No progress was made on marriage or our future life together. I lived in the present and enjoyed it. However, while I was in the present, her mind was visualizing her future. In her visualizations, I was missing in action. I had not made any decisions about the future house even though she mentioned it several times.

Several grandchildren were born into her family. With the appearance of each new grandchild, a month of time was cut off the portion of the year she was willing to spend away from her family and on hilltop dreamland. Eventually, the time was cut to precisely zero.

And me? I couldn't decide if I could leave Amish Country for the city. By the time I realized I would be willing to give up everything and move to her town, it was too late. I had once again waited too long.

Friends, don't wait too long in a relationship. Make decisions. Communicate your thoughts. Whether it's decisions about marriage, or plans for special things you want to do "someday" in retirement, or even simply letting your loved one know how much they mean to you—don't wait too long.

Pain and dejection await if you realize too late what you should have done long ago.

I failed both of us. And so I'm standing on an empty lot, alone again, and dreaming.

41

Butterfly

I'm still dreaming of a hilltop house filled with love and laughter, shared with a beautiful and godly lady. That dream has sustained me for over forty years. At times, dreams are all we have. But dreams do come true, don't they?

The greatest gift a man can receive is the love of a godly woman. I had it for a season. And I have yet to figure out the reason for that season.

I believe, though, that God works in everything for our good. And many times, we can't even see that good. The storm or the pain blinds us. Over the last agonizing months, the Holy Spirit has repeatedly reminded me that our marriage admittedly would have been difficult to work out.

I've wondered if the reason we were together in the first place was so that this book would be written. Through my grief, I heard the Spirit reminding me about the book my friend's late husband had wanted to write. The thing was, his ideas were along the same lines as a book I had always said I *should* write. Even before his widow had reached out to me, the Spirit had been prodding me for years to write some of what I have finally written here, now prompted by my time of pain.

Perhaps the reason God sent this worm into her life was to be rejected. Because of the rejection, I became encased in pain. Because of her rejection, I relied completely on the one who doesn't reject us—Jesus. Because of her rejection, I had to take a long, hard look at my life.

Jesus said the truth makes you free. The truth is now breaking the chrysalis of pain wrapped around me. The worm is no more. A new me is emerging.

I break out through the layers of pain, rejection, and devastation. I see the light of truth.

I will love again.

I will build a house on the hill.

There will be a beautiful, godly lady living there as well.

That will all happen because I will no longer wait too long!

She kissed a worm, and it turned into a butterfly and flew away.

Part 3
BECOMING ENOCH

42

Expiration Dates

You do know that you have an expiration date? Yes, your shelf life is limited.

Imagine the comments in the delivery room if we arrived in this world stamped with the last day of our earthly life: "Welcome to the world, little one. You will have 79 years." "This little one is set to expire at 25. Oh, how sad! That doesn't seem fair." "Who sets these dates, anyway?"

How silly. That doesn't happen. But ever since you and I were born, we have been living toward our expiration date. It would help us plan our lives if we knew when that would come. We could set up the seasons of our lives in an orderly fashion. But no one knows when they will have lived the final days of season four.

Well, perhaps there are exceptions. A prisoner about to be executed probably realizes he's about to expire. Consider this: The prisoner who knows that date may be more fortunate than many outside the prison walls. The prisoner sentenced to die realizes that time is precious and finite. I'm guessing he's more aware of the importance of choices in how he uses the hours or days he has left, even though his choices are limited. He also has the possibility of repenting and receiving eternal life if he chooses wisely.

Everyone outside the prison walls is also sentenced to die, but many are either drifting along with whatever current is carrying them or they are shackled by chains of indecision. Their expiration date arrives, and they have not used their allotted days well and are not prepared for eternity.

How sad. How foolish. Let's talk about the foolishness and danger of indecision.

When I was young, I had a thought. Upon reflection, it may be the most stupid thought I ever had. It ranks up there in the upper echelon of stupid, and if awards were given for foolish thoughts, I'd have a trophy sitting somewhere. (I'd be embarrassed to display it, of course.)

The thought that gains me the dubious honor was this: I thought perhaps I'd live as I pleased, and then just before gasping my final breath, I'd accept Jesus. Talk about high-stakes gambling. How could Mom and Dad have had such a foolish boy when they were so wise?

Sure, the thief on the cross had that opportunity, but how often does one get a chance to be crucified beside the Savior of the world? It's a rare event indeed. There are those few people we read about in the Bible who are brought back from the dead, and even today we occasionally hear the story of someone being declared dead but then they are revived. Surely those experiences change a person's perspective of the time they've been given, but these aren't everyday happenings. I don't think it's wise to count on having an extension granted.

I'm not a doctor, but I do have a prognosis for you. The news is not good. Your body is trapped in the gravitational pull of death. You are dying! Your expiration date is approaching, and you are already one day closer to dead than you were yesterday.

    I know a great healer. He heals the soul. Your body is doomed to decay, although God does have a plan for that, too. Your greater concern is your soul. On your expiration date, your soul enters either eternal life or eternal death.

    What if you actually knew the day you are set to expire? What would you do differently in the time you have left? Perhaps the changes you would make to live differently is how you should be living today.

    Don't wait too long. You do know you have an expiration date?

43

Enoch

Most of us know Methuselah as the oldest person ever to walk the face of the earth. His grandfather, Jared, was the second oldest ever. That must have been a mighty family tree.

The branch between them, though, the man who was Jared's son and Methuselah's father, only walked the earth for about one-third of the many years seen by these two very senior citizens. What happened? Why such a short life, such an early demise, between these two record-setting oldsters?

Perhaps we err in calculating Enoch's actual lifespan. Let's take a look.

Jared was 162 when his son was born. He named the boy Enoch. Apparently young Enoch started his family early, because he was only 65 when he became the father of Methuselah. Grandpa Jared was 227 when he held baby Methuselah.

About the time of Methuselah's birth, Enoch began a walk with God, and while Methuselah was growing up, his dad became known as something of a preacher. *Prophet,* they might have called him. Methuselah heard his dad warn people that God would judge those who lived wicked and ungodly lives. Rebellion against God's standards for living was already firmly entrenched in the family tree. Everyone had inherited a decidedly un-godly nature from Enoch's great-great-great-great-grandfather, Adam. Prophet Enoch also talked about the return of Jesus to judge the earth. Jude, the brother of Jesus, refers to those prophecies in the book of Jude, verse 14.

Enoch was preaching all this even before Noah started building his ark—one thousand years before!

The flood, by the way, seems to have changed the lifespan of human beings. Before the flood, life expectancy was around 800 years. Following the flood, the number stood at 300. When the earth opened up and all the springs poured forth, something happened to the years allotted to men. Did the canopy holding back those floodgates contribute to longer life?

We don't have the answer to that question. But let's get back to Enoch, the man for whom we can find no obituary among the many listed in the genealogies of Genesis 5.

When Jared was 527 years old, his son Enoch vanished. No one could find him.

I can imagine Jared going to his 300-year-old grandson Methuselah and asking the whereabouts of Enoch.

"I haven't seen him recently. Have you asked Mom where he is?" replied Methuselah.

Mrs. Enoch hadn't seen her husband either. He had been gone for several days. At first, she wasn't too concerned. Enoch enjoyed his walks every day. *God walks,* he called them. He came home inspired and shared with her what God had told him. He wasn't hesitant about telling others, too, what God had said—and it wasn't always what people wanted to hear. Sometimes, Mrs. Enoch was embarrassed for him; he could be so politically incorrect. He talked of things she could hardly imagine, things he said were coming someday. Mrs. Enoch had even heard her husband tell someone that God was pleased with him.

She was accustomed to Enoch spending so much time on those walks with God, but this time he had been gone longer than ever before, and she was concerned. She kept going to the kitchen window, checking the street, wondering when her husband would show up.

"Well," said Dad Jared, "if he doesn't return in a day or two, we will send out a search party."

They did send out that search party for young Enoch. Hebrews 11:5 tells us "he could not be found." Perhaps they nailed "Missing" posters at the city gate or tied "Have you seen this man?" flyers on vendor tables at the town market.

Enoch was reported lost and never found. In reality, he was translated. Translated from this world into another. God took him out of this world so he would not experience death.

Since he didn't actually die, wouldn't he be the oldest living person? Perhaps close to 5,000 years old?

Enough about life expectancies and genealogies. In a more serious vein, I'm compelled to ponder Enoch's relationship with God. Before Enoch vanished off the face of the earth, God commended him as one who pleased God (Hebrews 11:5).

Now, that's quite a recommendation. That's one I desire. Don't you? Is it still possible today to walk with God and have such a close relationship with our Creator? I believe it is.

An old story imagines Enoch and God taking frequent walks together. At times, they walked farther and farther in deep conversation. One day after a really long walk, God told Enoch, "We are closer to my home than yours. Just come home with me."

Isn't that an intriguing version of what may have happened?

I want to know what Enoch learned during those walks.

I started my own walk at about the same age as Enoch when he started walking with God. My walk took me over 2,000 miles on the Appalachian Trail. However, *walk* is a bit of a misnomer. It was a brutal slog through 300 valleys and difficult trudges over 300 mountains. God walked with me. (Although I sometimes joke that at times conditions were so horrible God stayed indoors and let me suffer alone.) A few years later, I walked over 500 miles across Spain on a famous route called the *Camino de Santiago.* That trail is a religious pilgrimage starting in France and winding all the way across northern Spain to the Atlantic Ocean. Several years ago, I hiked a trail in Israel called the Jesus Trail. That took me from Nazareth to Capernaum by the Sea of Galilee, where Jesus had His ministry headquarters.

In all these walks, I invited God to be my hiking partner and teach me lessons, things I needed to learn myself and truths I could pass on to others.

Some of those revelations were written in several books that have already been published with my name on the cover. The inspiration and power behind them, though, is God's. Many more of these lessons and truths have waited in the far recesses of my mind, anticipating the call that it's time to bring them forth and write them down.

Recently that call sounded. It took some time, because nothing I do happens easily. I tend to learn life's lessons the hard way. Just as the Appalachian Trail turned out to be far more difficult than I ever imagined, walking through life with God takes us over all kinds of terrain, through all kinds of weather, and with all kinds of pains and joys. This is how we learn the truths God has for us—by actually hiking the trail.

Now God, in His love and infinite wisdom, has allowed events to happen that have shaken and shattered me. What has happened also pushed me—pushed me to walk with Him more often, more closely, and with more of a listening ear than I have ever walked before.

44

Diverging Pathways

Enoch was relatively private about his talks with God. Although he spoke openly to his contemporaries, he recorded almost nothing for successive generations. An ancient book does bear his name, but most experts believe it was written a century or so before Jesus lived—and Enoch lived long before Noah and the flood.

David, though, wrote a great deal about his talks with God. I've already quoted many of his lines. His words sound familiar because they are words we've cried out ourselves. Words of praise and joy or words of desperation and anguish—David wrote them all. We read them, and we can feel what he's going through in his walk with God.

He ends Psalm 139 with this request: "Search me, God, and know my heart; test me and know my anxious thoughts. See if there is any offensive way in me, and lead me in the way everlasting."

David is asking two things of God as they walk and talk. He asks God to examine his thoughts and his heart. "Tell me your truths. Do my thoughts line up with yours? Where am I wrong? Straighten me out, Lord." You'll remember that he opened the psalm with the plea, "Create in me a clean heart." David wanted to know God's thoughts; he wanted God's mentoring. At another place, he wrote, "Keep me from deceitful ways," or, in another translation, "Keep me from lying to myself." David wanted God's truth concerning his character.

David also wanted literal guidance, God's GPS, if you will. "Lead me in the way everlasting." Is that your daily prayer?

You are on a pathway now, and it's headed toward a final and eternal destination. There are two possible pathways. Choose carefully. Don't float along without thinking about the path you're on, because the default path is the wrong one!

You are probably familiar with the poem by Robert Frost entitled, "The Road Not Taken." Frost wrote about coming to a point where two roads diverged. He needed to make a choice. After contemplation, he chose the road less traveled. It made a difference in the rest of his journey and in his destination.

The Bible speaks about two pathways. One is called the broad road. A large gate gives easy access to this well-traveled highway. This road looks most appealing; it welcomes all with promises of pleasures all along the way. Your guide on this path is the great deceiver, Satan. He won't appear as the cartoon devil with red horns and hooves. He will seem beautiful and charismatic. But beware. He's filled with evil on the inside, and he'll take you down the path that leads to an eternity separated from God.

This is the road we're all on—unless we determine to leave it and search for another gate leading to another road taking us to another destination.

This better pathway is less traveled, not as crowded. (That alone makes it more appealing to me.) The Bible calls this path the straight and narrow way. If you're interested in walking with God and getting insights into God's thoughts, you'll want this less-traveled path. If you want the pathway that leads to eternal life and joy—the "way everlasting" which David desired—then this is the gate and the path you will want to choose.

The narrow gate does require a radical decision. The glitzy, broad road has no requirements. You started life already on that road, and there's where you'll stay until you choose another path. The straight and narrow route does have requirements. You'll need to know the rules of the road, what you must do and know before being allowed access to what will be an incredible journey.

First off, you're not worthy to walk on this path, not even to go through the gate. You'll need to clean up. Many do not want to admit this, but this is truth. We have all failed. We all have a sickness unto death called sin.

Fortunately, there's an antidote for that disease. It's called Jesus.

This was Jesus' purpose in coming to earth: To let us know that God was offering us a way that would allow us to walk with Him as closely as Enoch did. Jesus opened that way for us, and all who believe in Jesus and come to Him for the antidote to the sin-disease will be qualified to walk with God. Jesus is our doorway to God. He provides the "cleaning up" that we need to do to walk in "the way everlasting."

This plan of God's is a gift. You know how simple it is to receive a gift from a friend—just accept it and be grateful. It's that easy to accept this gift. Many churches make it too difficult, but Romans 10:9-10 give the instructions:

> If you declare with your mouth, "Jesus is Lord," and believe in your heart that God raised him from the dead, you will be saved. For it is with your heart that you believe and are justified, and it is with your mouth that you profess your faith and are saved.

The requirements for this path are belief and a confession. Two bad guys were executed at the same time Jesus died on the cross. One of them, hanging there next to Jesus, simply asked Jesus to "remember me when you come into your kingdom." Those words tell me that he believed. That simple request was all it took for the thief to be admitted to Paradise. He probably had no idea Jesus would rise from the dead, but he believed Jesus was who He claimed to be.

That's not much different from what's required today. Our confession must be, "Jesus, I believe You are who You say You are. I believe You died for my sins. I believe You rose from the dead and are alive today. I wish to have a walk with You, finding out what that means for my life."

Then, my friend, you're ready for the journey on the way everlasting, the way to the life that is truly life. You don't want to wait to find this pathway. Do it now. Use David's prayer: "Lead me in the way everlasting."

45

God's Thoughts

Ever since I was a little boy and heard my dad read the account of Solomon asking for wisdom and understanding, I've prayed for wisdom. That seemed like a smart, sensible prayer. However, life so often got in the way, and being wise took a back seat to many other desires and pursuits. Has that happened to you, too?

Now I have determined to take walks with God and ask for His thoughts on life and living. I believe that was what God and Enoch discussed as they walked together. Enoch wanted to know what God had to say—about everything. In conversations, how often do we focus on ourselves, talking only about our own opinions and our personal concerns? Enoch was eager to listen and learn from his Creator.

In Psalm 139 verses 17-18, David says this about God: "How precious to me are your thoughts, O God. How vast is the sum of them! Were I to count them, they would outnumber the grains of sand."

Of course, the number of grains of sand on all the beaches of the world cannot be quantified. It's an incalculable number. If God has that many thoughts, He has no problem thinking thoughts about every man and woman on the planet. God's thoughts outnumber all of humanity.

God wants to make His thoughts available to sincere seekers. He is more than willing to take this deep spiritual walk with any person desiring it. He will even plant within us a special connection that helps us to hear and understand His thoughts. More about that later, but just know this: God wants this connection with us. He wants us to know what He's thinking.

As Enoch took those walks with God, I imagine him being delighted to discover God also wanted him to talk about all his opinions, concerns, and questions, too. Likewise, we will find God *does* want to hear from us. Of course, He knows it all already. We could try, but we'll never be able to hide any thoughts or worries from Him. He knows what's going on in our heart and head even before we do. So He doesn't *need* to ask what's on our mind. But He does want us to open up to Him. "Come and talk with me," He says (Psalm 27:8). Come. Ask your questions. Tell Him your thoughts. Vent your feelings.

He says, *Come, let's walk and talk.*

Mystery

I enjoy a good mystery story. The word *mystery* means *something secret or hidden*. It's a fact or matter that defies explanation. But it's only a mystery as long as it's actually unknown.

I enjoy unraveling and exposing mysteries. You wouldn't want to be seated beside me during a movie that involves a mystery. Halfway through the story, I'll turn to you and say, "He did it," or "She's not really dead."

When I was young, my cousin gave me a Hardy Boys mystery book. Many kids from my era grew up alongside these two sons of a detective named Fenton Hardy. Detective Hardy's two sons solved mysteries that baffled authorities, at times even solving a case Dad was working on. For us kids who were deprived of television and radio, these books were the ultimate in entertainment.

Now, so many years later, I can still recall names: grumpy Aunt Gertrude, their close friends Chet and Iola Morton, Biff Hooper, and others. The publishing company was Grosset and Dunlap. The writer was a Franklin W. Dixon; and as a boy,

I believed Franklin W. Dixon was the best writer who ever lived.

I read that first Hardy Boys book, and I was hooked on mysteries. I soon realized there were a series of Hardy Boys books. A local gift shop carried many of them. But books cost $1.25 back then, a fairly large sum for a young boy. I had, though, racked up quite a savings account in my young life. I had built it up to $5.00.

I marched into my bank, handed my savings book to the teller, and requested a withdrawal of $1.25. With money in hand, I entered the gift shop and excitedly picked up the next book in the series. I still recall how I felt as I approached the cashier, cradling that precious blue hardcover book.

She rang up my purchase and announced the total was $1.29. I quickly pointed out her error. "It says here $1.25."

That was my first introduction to state sales tax. I had never in my young years heard of such highway robbery. The lady said she would overlook the tax for that time only. "If you buy another book, the total will be $1.29." I sincerely hope that lady didn't spend any time incarcerated for eliminating the tax that day.

However, I doubted I would return anytime soon. My savings had dipped below $4.00. I would need a few more years of saving nickels and dimes to get it built up again.

Oh yes, a business plan soon emerged!

In school, I shared with my six friends my excitement about these great mystery stories. I soon made them an offer: for twenty-five cents, they could read my book. Twenty-five cents per person.

Several balked at the price, until I presented another option: If they bought the next book, I would pay them twenty-five cents to read their copy. Fortunately, no one called my bluff. I would have had to make another savings withdrawal to pay the reading fee.

I was now running a for-profit enterprise. After collecting $1.50 from my book club, I'd head back to the gift shop for the next book in the series. I'd have a new book and 21 cents toward rebuilding my savings account. I was well on my way to becoming a wealthy capitalist.

I still have the collection of Hardy Boys books that were purchased at a grand total of $1.25.

More than fifty years passed, and I learned more about my beloved books. I discovered that the Dunlap partner in the publishing company was a gentleman from a neighboring community. George T. Dunlap was born in Orrville, Ohio, and was instrumental in the founding of the local hospital named after him. I also discovered who Franklin W. Dixon was—and who he wasn't.

I was doing a book signing event in Florida. A tour bus arrived and disgorged 35 northern folks in search of sunshine. An elderly lady approached my table and inspected my books. She remarked that her dad had been a writer himself.

"Anyone I might know?" I asked.

"Have you ever read any Hardy Boys books?"

Had I ever! "Yes, of course. My favorite reading growing up. The author was Franklin W. Dixon."

"That was my dad," she said.

My jaw dropped, and I almost slid out of my chair to the floor.

"Are you serious? You have no idea how your dad impacted my life."

She continued. "There were evenings around the supper table when my dad would talk about a mystery he was working on. We'd always want to know what happens next. Dad would say, 'I don't know yet. I haven't written it yet.'"

I was fascinated with this glimpse into my first favorite author's life. But then I was told the truth about Franklin W. Dixon.

He didn't exist.

He was a ghostwriter. A ghostwriter is someone with writing talents who will write a book for you. You get to put your name on the book and pretend you did it yourself. This is often done for movie stars and politicians who have an ego but no writing ability.

This woman's father was not only a ghostwriter, but he was one ghost among many ghosts. Franklin W. Dixon was a pseudonym for numerous writers working for a man named Edward Stratemeyer. These writers collaborated together on other book series as well. Some of you have certainly read Nancy Drew books. Same company, another one of the ghosts. The Nancy Drew writer's ghostly name was Carolyn Keene. For you Tom Swift fans, Victor Appleton was your ghost writer. (Yes, I also bought and leased out Tom Swift books at twenty-five cents a read.) Finally, I'm sure some of you recall reading a series about the Bobbsey twins. Surprise, surprise. Another ghost appears, this one by the name of Laura Lee Hope.

Be assured, there's no mystery involved in my writings. I am who my name on the cover says I am. I'm not a ghost. I do, however, have a ghost (of sorts) who resides within me. The Holy Ghost.

Wow. That does sound odd. I prefer "Holy Spirit."

There is a far greater mystery than the mystery stories I've been remembering. The originator of this great story is the original mystery writer. He was the creator of this genre of stories, centered on a mystery called "The Mystery of the Divine Presence." Like me sitting in a theater and unraveling a mystery for anyone sitting next to me, the apostle Paul explains this "secret" God kept hidden for ages but now unveils for all who will believe:

> To them God has chosen to make known among the Gentiles the glorious riches of this mystery, which is Christ in you, the hope of glory. (Colossians 1:27)

I will need my Ghost writer within to assist me as we unravel this mystery.

47

The Interpreter

"I know exactly what you're thinking…"

How often have you said that to your spouse or a good friend? In an intimate friendship, we get to know the other person so well that we do know how they think.

Have you ever said the same thing to God?

"My thoughts are not your thoughts. My ways are not your ways." These are God's words, given through the prophet Isaiah (see Isaiah 55:8). If we want to walk with God and hear what He has to say, how can our human minds comprehend the thoughts of God?

Some of you are just starting off on the narrow way; others have been journeying along it for decades. But at the very start, the moment you walk through the gate, you are given another amazing gift. You'll be given a companion for the journey—the Holy Spirit.

This companion will be your guide and provide many things for you. We will talk about Him more throughout this book, but here's the thing to know now—He will interpret for you. All God has to say to you will flow through the one who understands God's mind and His ways. You *can* know God's thoughts, because His Holy Spirit will always be with you to help you understand.

1 Corinthians 2:6-16 describes what happens. God had a secret wisdom that was destined for us before recorded time began. Remember, as you walk this path with God, you are a part of the plan He had in place before He even created the world. That plan existed before time, and the plan goes beyond the end of time. No eye has seen or heard what God has prepared for us at the end of the narrow road, in the celestial city.

Paul inserts the comment that if the rulers at the time of Jesus' death had understood all this, they would not have killed Him. I suppose it is to our great advantage that they didn't understand—if Jesus had not been killed, we would not have this adventurous, narrow road to travel.

We also would not have our Guide. When Jesus was preparing His disciples for His departure from this world, He told them that He needed to leave so the Spirit of truth could come. That is the Holy Spirit. And the Spirit of truth is available to everyone around the globe. "When the Spirit of truth comes," Jesus told them (and us), "He will guide you into all truth. He'll speak what He hears from God." (See John 16:13)

Those thoughts of God, more numerous than the grains of sand on earth's beaches, can be revealed to us through the Holy Spirit of truth. The passage in 1 Corinthians 2 explains it this way: Our human thoughts are understood by us humans. Each person knows his or her own thoughts. The Holy Spirit knows and understands God's "deep thoughts" because He is the Spirit of God. In turn, the Spirit, living with us, reveals and explains those thoughts to us.

These are spiritual truths in spiritual words. I call them "God thoughts." To the folks on the broad road, this is all foolishness and makes no sense at all. Their guide is described in Scripture as the "spirit of this world."

But God chose us to be a part of His grand scheme in both time and eternity, and He makes His truth available to us. He's even sent us love letters. We've called it the Bible.

When my wife and I were dating, we used to exchange letters. (For the younger generation reading this, google "letter writing." There are actually tutorials and videos on "How to write a letter.") I looked forward to every one of her letters and read them with eagerness and attention. I loved her and wanted to know everything I possibly could about her. I lived with her and loved her for more than thirty years, and I knew what her answer would be to almost any question I'd ask her. I could hear her voice, even when she was no longer on this earth. I knew what she would say in almost any situation.

In the same way, we love God, our Creator, and want to know everything we can about Him. We read His love letter, and our Guide, the Spirit, helps us to understand what God is saying. Jesus was God, here as a human being. Jesus was also a love letter, sent to tell us much more about who God is. We get to know Him better and better, and our Guide, the Spirit, reminds us of what Jesus taught. The more we get to know God the Father, Jesus the Son, and the Holy Spirit, the more we tune into those thoughts of God.

Did Enoch actually walk with the bodily form of God? Of course not. We are told no one has seen God. However, Enoch walked with the Spirit of God, and he was given access to the thoughts and knowledge of God.

We walk this narrow pathway with a Guide who interprets God's thoughts for us. God desires that each of us will have a deep, intimate love relationship with our Creator, learning to know Him and His truths, learning to hear His thoughts. As we walk closely with Him, listen to our Interpreter, and talk with Him, there might very well be times when we can say, "I know exactly what You're thinking!"

48

Knowing the Holy Spirit

The narrow way isn't always an easy way. You will need to depend on your Guide, the Holy Spirit living within you.

Do you know this guide for your journey?

It's easier to walk with someone you know than with a perfect stranger. Knowing a person means you have defined their character and personality traits. Walking beside a stranger is quite different; you see him, you're aware he is there, but you don't really *know* anything about him.

That's the only awareness many people have of the Holy Spirit—as a mysterious presence we can't really relate to or know. Shouldn't we know more about the personality of this divine presence who lives and travels with us?

Personality? Indeed, the Holy Spirit has a personality. Some people view the Holy Spirit as only a powerful influence. This thinking leads to constantly wanting more of the Spirit. However, if we think of the Spirit as a divine Person, our thinking turns to asking how we can give more of ourselves to Him, how we can live more fully in and by the Spirit.

The Holy Spirit is as real as God the Father and Jesus the Son. Understanding what it means to have this divine Person residing in our hearts will humble us.

Who is He? Can we know Him? Let's look at the characteristics of His personality as described in the Bible.

The Holy Spirit has will or determination. He determines what gifts each of us has. If you doubt that, read 1 Corinthians 12:1-11. Some receive wisdom, some get knowledge, some are given the gift of prophecy. Other gifts are mentioned as well. You may be blessed with several of these gifts. Verse 11 tells us the Holy Spirit gives them to us *as He determines.* He decides.

We often hear about the love of God. We sing the songs "Jesus Loves Me" and the wonderful favorite "The Love of God." Are you aware the Holy Spirit also loves you? In Romans 15:30, Paul talks about the love of the Spirit. Love is an emotion. That's certainly a character trait ascribed to personality.

Our salvation is tied to the Holy Spirit just as closely as it is to Jesus Christ and God. In John 3, that chapter well known for its passage about being born again, Jesus said our new birth is from the Spirit. The new life we're given is nurtured and sustained by the Spirit, and it is by the power of the Spirit that we will someday be resurrected! In Romans 8 and Galatians 5, Paul goes into detail about how walking with this Guide can change our everyday lives. There is no part of our lives where the Spirit does not stay involved, unless, of course, we shut Him out.

And we can do that. We can say "No" to the Holy Spirit. This brings Him sorrow. Did you know the Holy Spirit grieves? Many of us have grieved, and whatever the reason for our grief, it's a painful process. The Spirit grieves, too, when we open the door to attitudes and actions not worthy of children of God (see Ephesians 4:30). This divine Person dwelling in the temple of our bodies sees every action, hears every word, and knows every thought. Do you really want to be selfish or unkind? Do you want to fill His temple in your heart with bitterness and grudges? Do you want foul language coming out of your mouth? Those actions grieve the Holy Spirit.

Finally, here's the really good part. It's from Romans 8 verses 12-17. Letting our Guide show the way will free us from our old human nature, the part of us constantly fighting against God's way. Those led by the spirit of God are sons and daughters of God. We are called God's children! And the Holy Spirit will be right there, reassuring and encouraging us when the deceiver slips in and starts whispering doubt into our ears. The Spirit is our strongest ally!

Get to know your Guide. The more you know Him, the closer you will want to walk with Him as you enjoy the adventure of an amazing journey.

49

The Counselor's Residence

When Jesus talked about His departure, He reassured His disciples, "I won't leave you like orphans. I'm going to give you a Counselor to be with you."

A counselor is a person trained to give guidance on whatever issue you might be dealing with. We're familiar with legal counselors, financial counselors, marriage counselors, family counselors, and many other people who supposedly are "specialists" in certain areas.

The Holy Spirit is this counselor Jesus promised, sent to those willing to love Jesus and obey His teachings. In John 14:23, Jesus says that if anyone loves Him, God will love them, too, and "we will come to him and make our home with them."

On my hike across Spain on the Camino de Santiago, I stopped and marveled at many of the old and elaborate cathedrals. One in particular inspired me. I had ended this day in Leon, Spain, where the imposing cathedral Pulchra Leonina beckoned me to enter. This cathedral has 125 stained-glass windows located high in the walls and ceiling. I was enraptured as I strolled about, gazing upward at the beautiful streams of colored lights flowing from the stained glass. I described it then as shimmering, glimmering beams of deep color dancing all about me.

That is describing us. That's our cathedral (or temple) when the Holy Spirit comes and dwells within.

Many of us have been beaten down by loss: a marriage gone wrong, a job suddenly stripped away, a spouse slipping away to Heaven, loss of dreams, loss of love. So many painful events in our lives. So much painful rehabilitation needed. Our hearts are like glass that someone may have dropped, carelessly or accidentally. The glass has shattered into so many pieces we wonder if we can even find them all again.

The devil may say it's broken glass, it can't be repaired, you've lost everything. He is so wrong! God can repair broken-glass lives. He takes those shards stained with our pain and pieces them together to create a thing of beauty. The stained-glass heart is a masterpiece by the greatest Creator.

The difference between us and the cathedral in Leon is that in stained-glass lives, the light flows outward. The most wise and important Counselor has come to live within this cathedral, and the glory of His presence sends a luminance into the darkness around us.

Our bodies are a temple of the Holy Spirit (1 Corinthians 6:19), our Counselor of truth, sent by God. For the arrival of such an important counselor, you certainly would want your house clean and in order.

Imagine entering a beautiful cathedral with a bag of dirt and intentionally tossing the dirt around, desecrating the beautiful edifice. Imagine emptying bags of garbage all over the pews and floor and altar.

You certainly don't want to have garbage littering your bodily temple where the Holy Spirit has taken up residence. However, many do just that.

Keep your temple clean. The enemy of God's plans would love to see us desecrating the Holy Spirit's temple. Satan tempts us with all kinds of garbage—but be on guard, because he usually disguises the garbage as pleasurable and desirable. As one example, pornography lures and offers potent promises, but it's destructive. It's devilish. It destroys marriages and relationships. You cannot sit in front of a computer imbibing such garbage and still keep clean the temple of the Counselor of truth.

In such a scenario, can you imagine the pain of your Holy Counselor as you insist on breaking more pieces of your life?

50

Prayer Guide

For many years, I did not have a powerful prayer life. I didn't even understand what "a powerful prayer life" actually meant or what it could be. I was spiritually lazy.

Then God allowed me to go through this wilderness devastation by the loss of a relationship I trusted, and the intense pain pushed me to go searching for God. Suffering deeply from this rejection, I wanted to hear from God. I wanted to know His thoughts. I went to the Scriptures, hoping for some balm for my wounds. As I searched the Scriptures, I also read books on prayer.

Do you ever kneel to pray and feel like your prayer goes nowhere? I have.

Do you ever question whether God even hears your prayers? I have.

There certainly are times when we don't feel like praying, and those are times we need to pray more than ever.

During this time, I discovered a volume of sermons by R. A. Torrey. Torrey wrote a few lines that changed my prayer life, and I'd like to share his insight with you. This could change your life, as well.

The secret to a dynamic prayer life is found in Ephesians 2:18. There, Paul tells us we can come to God through the Holy Spirit because of what Jesus did for us. But what does it really mean to come to God through the Holy Spirit? Torrey offered an explanation of this, and as I said, it changed my prayer life.

Torrey wrote that when we are ready to pray, it's the work of the Holy Spirit to take us figuratively by the hand and lead us into the very presence of God. The Spirit introduces us to the Almighty, and He makes God real to us as we pray.

We've been given a special connection to God! It's a wonderful mystery!

Now when I kneel to pray, I tell the Holy Spirit that I need to speak to God. "Take me there, please," and I wait quietly until I feel I'm in the presence of God.

It's real. The Spirit works. Try it. Your prayer life will change.

51

Lonely Places to Pray

My grandfather was an Old Order Amish farmer. He was a man who early in life discovered what it meant to be in Jesus and to have Jesus in him. He had invited the Holy Spirit to dwell within him. He desired to hear those spiritual thoughts God has promised to give through the Holy Spirit.

He was a man of intense prayer. Behind his house, he had a "prayer tree." It bordered his and a neighboring property, and he would often get out of bed in the middle of the night to go outside and pray by that tree. It was his lonely place to pray. One night he walked out, the door shut behind him, and he immediately realized he had locked himself out. He prayed, tried the door handle, and it opened!

The day came that the neighbor cut down the tree, not knowing its value to my granddad. Grandfather was devastated. However, that didn't deter him from his prayer sessions. I don't know if he continued to pray by the tree stump or found another lonely place, but I do know he prayed all his life. He especially prayed that all ten of his children would come to know the saving grace of Jesus.

That prayer was answered.

Jesus often withdrew to pray in lonely places (Luke 5:16). In Mark 1, He got up very early in the morning while it was still dark and again sought out a solitary place to pray. It would seem that a solitary place would be easy to find that early in the morning. Simon and a few buddies finally found Him and exclaimed, "Everybody is looking for you." It must have been quite a solitary place. Maybe by a tree somewhere?

In Luke 6, we read that Jesus went to a mountainside and prayed all night. Just a few verses after this, Luke describes how a great number of people from the area came to Him for healing and to be freed from demons because "power was coming from him and healing them all" (Luke 1:19).

Interesting. You would think that Jesus would have the power ready and always available. He was divine, was He not? However, I wonder if it required those lonely-place prayer sessions with His Father God for Jesus to have that power. At several places in the gospels we read that power "came out of" Jesus. We cannot give out spiritually what we don't take in. During those times of prayer, Jesus was communicating with God and being filled with powerful spiritual thoughts and healing powers. The deep relationship with His Father guided Jesus' life. He said that He only spoke what the Father told Him to speak, the works He did were done by the Father living in Him, and He could do nothing on His own.

For Jesus, doing the Father's will and accomplishing what He was sent to do was the "food" that carried Him through His days (John 4:34). He needed those extended, uninterrupted times of communication with God.

So do we, walkers on the narrow way. If you want to hear the thoughts of God, seek out your own lonely place and pray.

52

God Speaking

We have no way of knowing how Enoch heard God's thoughts and words. A more important question to ask is if we are listening for His voice speaking to us today.

How does God speak? A gentleman called me one evening. He had read *Hiking Through* and was curious how I knew I was hearing from God. A Christian man in his mid-seventies, he said he wasn't aware he had ever heard from God.

The "wasn't aware" is what caught my attention.

I remarked to him that he certainly had heard from God.

"Do you read your Bible?"

Yes, certainly he did.

"Those are God's love letters to you. When you read those verses, God is speaking to you."

We have God's promise that He has come to live with us in the Holy Spirit, who will reveal His mysteries and thoughts; yet many have never really developed a relationship with our Guide on the narrow pathway.

We have eyes to see, yet we often don't see everything around us that is God's blessing on us.

We have ears to hear, but we may not stop to hear the symphony of nature God has composed for us.

We have human intelligence to discern and solve many of life's mundane problems, yet our thoughts do not push beyond earthly boundaries.

And so, in times of distress when we plod through the valley or the wilderness, sometimes we ask, "Where are you, oh God?"

Sometimes, it's easier to look back. When we reflect on difficult times, we see obvious signposts from God that we either missed completely or dismissed as insignificant.

But if our relationship with the Holy Spirit, Jesus, and God is blooming and growing, we will see those signposts guiding us through these deep valleys. I haven't always "heard" God speaking. I often asked for signs, and even then, I sometimes missed the signs or dismissed the Spirit's counsel and went off in the wrong direction. God loves us, though, and He'll redirect if we're willing to follow our Guide.

53

Signs from God

It was probably the first time in my life that I thought about and started to look for signs from God. Following my wife's funeral, my pastor made a statement to me that soon became truth. He said, "Look for signs from God that are just for you. Little messages from Him to remind you that He is in control and your loved one is well." He assured me that these signs would be evident if I was observant and open to them. From years of officiating at funerals, he knew that God works in this way.

But I had never thought much about this before and wondered, *Does God really do that?*

It wasn't long before I began to see how right my pastor was. As a matter of fact, that very night I experienced a comforting message from God.

I had just returned from the funeral. The doorbell rang, and on my doorstep stood an Amish lady, one of Mary's best friends. During our long years of fighting cancer, this friend had often come to the house to help care for Mary.

She held a vase filled with flowers, and in the bouquet was one stem with a chrysalis attached. She had found it in her garden and remembered how much Mary loved watching monarch butterflies hatch and then releasing them to fly away.

I thanked her for the lovely gesture, but did not plan to tend that chrysalis the way Mary had. Knowing that one of my sisters had never seen a butterfly emerging, I planned to take the chrysalis to her house the next day. She could tend and watch it.

God and the butterfly had other plans.

That evening, I fell asleep in my recliner in the living room. At 2:00 AM, I awoke. The overhead light was still on, and I could hear a rustling sound above me. To my amazement, a monarch butterfly was circling above, around the light on the ceiling. It had broken the bonds constricting it and struggled free to become the beautiful creature God planned for it to be.

The butterfly made ever larger swoops around the room but always returned to the light. Mary's butterflies had always been birthed in a jar; this one had emerged into the relative freedom of my kitchen and living room. But I doubted a butterfly would make a good house pet. I wanted to set it free.

I knew I wouldn't be able to catch it. But I noticed that it was attracted to light, so I turned on the kitchen light and turned off the living room light. The little Wanderer followed the light to the kitchen. I turned on the light in the foyer, and turned off the kitchen light. The butterfly again followed the light. I opened the front door and turned on the porch light. The foyer light snapped off and that little critter winged its way to the great outdoors.

"Look for signs from God that all is well."

That was what happened just hours after I buried my wife. The caterpillar inside that chrysalis had transformed, followed the light, and found freedom. My wife, too, had broken her bonds and followed the light, entering into her eternal freedom, transformed into who God had planned for her to be.

If your journey has been hard and you wonder if God knows or cares about what's happening to you, pray for confirmation that He indeed does. He answers those prayers. He still speaks. He wants to communicate with you. Look for those little reminders that He loves and cares about you.

54

Don't Wait

About one year after my wife passed away, I felt a restlessness settling in. This concerned my job and the direction in which my life was going. The life I had known with Mary was gone. You cannot "put your life back together" when you have lost a spouse. Yes, I still had my family, dearer than ever to me. But I was floundering, not knowing how to build this new life. I prayed about the possibility of a new direction.

One day, while reading the obituaries (a habit I picked up from my dad), I came across one that required several columns. This dearly departed man had lived a full life—that is, if you define a full life as keeping busy. He was a member of many business and social clubs. He had been recognized for many achievements in his world of business. The description of his endeavors commanded two full columns.

I wondered if he had any time at all to spend with his family or to spend intimate time in a rich walk with God. I didn't know him, so I could only imagine. And from the long report of his busyness, I imagined he did not. As I reflected on his life, though, I recognized that I wasn't having a close Enoch walk with God either. That day, I realized we can let life events dictate the outcome of our obituary, or we can write our own obituary. We have the power.

One day, folks would be reading a column about me. I imagined what my obituary might include: the facts of a restaurant-management career, church membership, familial connections. What else? What else was there to say, at that point in my life?

Then I considered what I wanted my obituary to say. That wording included dreams I had of hiking the Appalachian Trail and writing a book. Today, I'd word it like this: "Paul took walks with God, and God commended him for being pleasing to Him."

These thoughts led me to two determinations: My obituary was going to be interesting reading! And, for that to happen, I had to have the courage to make difficult life changes.

You see, there were many things in my life I regretted. Many regrets concerned my family. I'd been a workaholic, chasing career and financial goals. Those goals aren't necessarily a bad thing, but when they interfere with your walks with your family and your God, it's time to reassess. My children were grown. My wife was gone. It was too late to spend more time with little ones and too late to be the kind of husband I always thought I *would* be—until I got too busy.

I waited too long. Until my imaginary obituary was staring me in the face, I did not see it was time to seize the power we have, the power to write our obituaries.

From someone who knows the price we pay for not appreciating and loving our families right now, this very day that we have—please heed the message: Don't wait. Any waiting "until tomorrow" is waiting too long.

55

Making Hard Choices

Eighteen months after my wife, Mary, passed away from cancer, I would have told you I had passed through all the stages of grief, yet I was still unsettled. I was still asking, *Where were you, God, when Mary died?* Perhaps He was there, perhaps He wasn't. In my internal debates, I could have made a case for either argument. Perhaps there was no meaning to her death except that it was her time to go. Why do bad things happen to good people? That question has been asked over and over. I've not yet heard an answer that satisfies.

I do know, however, that God can bring good out of bad situations. Because of Mary's death, I became an author. I write words that have the power to change lives.

I had a sense it was time to leave my position at the restaurant, yet I was too young to retire. A man has to have a purpose in life, a reason to get out of bed in the morning. What would get me out of bed if I no longer had a job?

I enjoy hiking. Over the years, I had read just about every book written about the Appalachian Trail. I'd often dream about the possibility of hiking the A.T. someday. This isn't a weekend hike, or even one accomplished during a vacation. The rugged trail stretches 2,176 miles through fourteen states from Georgia to Maine. It normally requires six months to complete the hike. The challenge of this hike kept calling to me.

I could almost imagine a phone call to my director of operations.

"Hello… You need what? You're doing what?"

"You heard right," I'd reply. "I'm not feeling the best; I need to call off a few days."

"That shouldn't be a problem. How many days do you need?"

"I was thinking… around 180 days."

Well, I knew *that* wasn't going to happen.

If I was going to hike the Appalachian Trail, I would have to walk away from my job. Since Mary's death, the responsibilities I had at the restaurant were the only thing giving my life structure. My family had given me comfort, but they all had their own lives. My life and my dreams for the future had all vanished with Mary. The only thing I had left was the daily routine of work. What would my life be if I walked away from family and had no job to force me to go through each day?

And a question kept coming back to mind: Wouldn't it be totally irresponsible for me to leave a secure job and go off into the wilderness for six months? My upbringing had instilled hard work, common sense, and responsibility in my brain.

I was poised on the brink of making a decision that was totally unheard of and unimagined in my world. Even I could not quite envision such a drastic change in life's direction.

So I did what I highly recommend to you: I prayed for a sign from God. I wanted an unmistakable signal from Him that I should take this preposterous step.

When I finally decided to retire early from my restaurant-management career, I would not have imagined what God had in store for me. God took a man in a restaurant who fed thousands of people a day and turned him into a writer who feeds thousands of people with written words.

However, there were hard times and hard choices along the way, and I needed God's confirmation that I was going in the right direction.

There is just one warning if you sincerely pray for God's guidance. You may very well be surprised—shocked, even—at God's answer. He knows how entrenched we are in our thinking and our day-to-day life, and He'll often need to do something extreme to break us out of the confines of thinking and behavior we've built around us.

At least, that's what He did to me.

56

Answered Prayer

I was in my office at the restaurant when my pager sounded. "You are needed in the booth room. An irate customer doesn't like his chicken." In spite of his complaint, I discovered this man had already been to the buffet three times and had consumed nearly an entire chicken.

Approaching the customer, I sensed danger. A sweaty face, bulging with veins, swiveled toward me. The short, stocky man was missing a neck and presented the perfect image of steroid-induced, weightlifting excess.

"What's the problem, sir?"

"This chicken isn't any good."

"Just this one piece, or the ten that preceded it? I am aware you've already made three trips to the buffet and returned to your booth with plates loaded with our delicious fried chicken."

"Are you calling me a liar?" he bellowed. His petite wife cowered opposite him.

For a moment, I ignored all I'd been taught about "The customer is always right." I even swept aside "The customer isn't always right, yet he's always the customer." Who comes up with that drivel? Obviously, someone in a front office somewhere who's never actually managed people or dealt with thousands of customers daily.

I did what every manager on the face of the earth has wanted to do at one time or another. I spoke truth to a bully customer. "Yes, you are a liar," I replied.

That lit a fuse in the no-neck chicken eater. "I could kill you," he screamed.

We now had quite an audience watching and listening to the display of the restaurant manager's new approach to customer service. Some were nodding approvingly, giving me the courage to continue.

"I suppose you could kill me—if you could catch me. However, in your condition, you could never catch me."

"What do you mean, 'condition'?"

"Steroids," I muttered, looking to the approving crowd. "You wouldn't be fast enough, with your belly full of chicken."

"I'm leaving here and never coming back!" he shouted.

I shouted in return, pointing at him. "That's too soon!" and I turned around and walked away.

Back in the safety of my office, I reflected on my newfound approach to customers—pure, raw honesty. I couldn't say I was proud of my performance in that hour, but I also would not admit that I wasn't. I doubted the main office would consider changing our employee handbooks to embrace my more liberal approach to customer satisfaction.

Foremost in my mind was the realization that something within me was changing. I had been praying about leaving my job. "God, give me some sign that it's time to leave this job."

I repeat my warning: Don't ever ask for signs unless you are very serious. They will come. Often, God's answer is not even close to what we imagined or expected.

I would have preferred a soft, gentle sign. You know, one I could ignore if it wasn't quite what I wanted. Or one I could possibly rationalize away with doubts that I'd heard correctly. The signs I received couldn't be ignored or brushed away.

The daily stresses were taking a toll. It was also evident in my attitude toward my co-workers. Small things stressed over by my employees boggled my mind. How could such trivial matters mean so much to their lives? They couldn't begin to comprehend what real loss and pain were. I knew. I was grieving such a great loss. But their overreactions to such insignificant matters received no sympathy from me. I was only irritated and impatient with their lack of discernment on what was important and what was inconsequential.

The morning following the confrontation of the no-neck chicken eater, another sign appeared. As I was running the cash register at the front counter, a middle-aged man stood to my left, obviously waiting on me. When he had my attention, he began his complaint.

"Your bacon's not good this morning."

"What do you mean, 'not good'?"

"It's too thin, and it's greasy."

"Sounds quite like it should be," replied the manager.

"You're not hearing me. It doesn't taste good. It's too greasy."

"Oh, I hear you, sir. We are talking pig fat here. Pork bellies. Grease. Yum, yum. Here's what I'll do. I'll take that up with the pigs. See if I can get them to produce less greasy pig fat."

With that, I solved another customer complaint. It seemed I was building my new customer-service resume.

As I've said before, I've always had to learn life's lessons the hard way. First, God began nudging me; He stirred the restlessness in my soul. I'd gone on in my usual direction in spite of what I was feeling. Then God cranked up the volume and sent these harsh, jarring messages that it was time to make changes. But still I wavered.

Shortly after these two encounters, I visited my wife's grave for some one-on-one conversation with her. I also stopped in occasionally to inspect a portion of my real estate holdings. I own the small parcel of real estate directly beside Mary's resting place.

"It's me again, Mary. What to do, what to do?"

"You sound troubled," came a voice in my mind, that voice I knew so well.

"I asked God for signs that it's time to leave the restaurant, and all I get is irate customers and more stress at work with all these silly employee issues."

"Don't you see it? Those are the signs you asked for."

"But what would I do if I quit my job?"

"Go follow your dreams."

"My dreams? The only thing I'm dreaming about these days is the Appalachian Trail."

"Exactly. Go do it."

"But it doesn't make sense to quit a good, high-paying job at age 57."

"Then you should probably do it."

"It *would* make good obituary reading, wouldn't it?"

Don't get to the end of your life and wonder "What if...?" Don't write a boring obituary. Follow your dreams.

If God is answering your prayers for guidance on a matter, pay attention.

And don't wait too long.

57

Signpost #91

The story of Signpost #91 begins on the day Mary and I received the devastating news that her cancer was stage 4 and had already spread to her lymph nodes and to her liver.

"How much time do we have, doctor?" I needed to know.

"It depends on how she reacts to treatment, but possibly a few months to a few years."

What does one do after such terrible news has slashed its way into your life?

I reached for my Bible and opened it at random. Psalm 91 was on the page before me.

"Whoever dwells in the shelter of the Most High will rest in the shadow of the Almighty. I will say of the LORD, 'He is my refugee and my fortress, my God, in whom I trust,'" I read aloud to Mary.

Mary took great comfort in the final few verses of the psalm that talk about being blessed with long life if we call upon Him in time of trouble. In trouble. Were we ever!

At the time of that first reading of Psalm 91, I was not yet aware that God had given me a signpost for my pilgrimage through my valley of weeping. With the passing of time, I saw that He had, and I began to look for the signs.

Mary read Psalm 91 every day for the rest of her life; and four years later, our pastor used the psalm at her memorial service.

On March 31, 2008, the morning I began my Appalachian Trail hike in Georgia, my scheduled Bible reading was Psalms 91. I did not choose it. It just "happened" that way.

My backpack was heavy with everything I needed to live out a five-month hike in the woods. My tent would be my abode for many of those nights. As I read my devotional that morning, it was comforting to read the chapter so familiar and precious to Mary. Verse 10, though, was meant for me on that day and in that place. I was stunned to read the promise that if I made the Most High my dwelling, then no harm or disaster would come near my tent!

Signpost #91 kept appearing along the trail, a reminder that God had things under control.

Every year, the Appalachian Trail Conservancy keeps a record of how many hikers attempt a thru-hike and how many actually finish it. A thru-hike is when a hiker walks the entire length of the Appalachian Trail in one year. In most years, about two thousand hikers attempt to do this. It's an extremely difficult trek through 300 valleys and over 300 mountains. Only 20 percent accomplish the goal and finish.

I signed my name to a registry that first day of my hike. I was Hiker #391 leaving Georgia, headed for Maine.

The headquarters for the Appalachian Trail is in Harpers Ferry, West Virginia. The trail runs through this town and hikers stop in at the headquarters to have a photo taken for a yearbook of all hikers attempting the thru-hike. Any hiker getting this far on the trail is almost halfway to the final goal at the top of Mt. Katahdin in Maine.

My photo was taken and inserted into the yearbook. I was hiker #191 heading north. I had somehow passed 200 other hikers who had either quit or were slower than I.

The final day arrived. August 13, 2008. I had reached the foothills of Mount Katahdin in Baxter State Park in Maine. I approached the ranger station where thru-hikers were required to sign in. I signed the register as "Apostle, hiking from Georgia to Maine."

I was hiker # 91 heading up the mountain to the finish of my hike.

There it was, the signpost from God as I was about to finish my pilgrimage.

It was as if God whispered to me, "Mary is fine. Go finish the hike and go home and write the message I gave you to write."

58

Writing Your Book?

I did what God asked of me. I returned home and wrote a book called *Hiking Through*. When it was released, an amazing thing happened. People responded! Because I was faithful to what God asked of me, God has used the book as a signpost for many other hurting people.

Over the course of the next few years, several thousand letters and emails poured in. Most of the writers wanted to tell me how the book had affected their lives.

One email said, *We were contemplating a divorce. We stopped to refuel at a Flying J truck stop, and your book was on a rack there. We purchased it, and our marriage was saved.*

A gentleman in a hospital gift shop was browsing through a book rack. He accidentally bumped the rack and it collapsed, spilling the books onto the floor. He returned all the books to their position, but as he turned to leave, one book again fell to the floor. It was *Hiking Through*. He took this as a sign he was to purchase the book. He did so. Outside the entrance to the hospital, he happened upon a young man in desperate straits. The young man was hopelessly depressed.

"I'm planning to kill myself," he said. The gentleman offered him *Hiking Through* and urged the young man to read it before taking such drastic action. The young man agreed and took the book. I've often wondered about the ending of that story, but I believe God's hand was in every step, from the moment the gentleman entered the gift shop.

A man from a New England state emailed me one day. He was a Catholic man who had left his faith. At a Walmart, he saw *Hiking Through* on a book rack. This man loved hiking, so he took the book home and found—much to his surprise and frustration—that it was a book with a spiritual message. He was about to return the book but at the last minute determined to give it a chance. It brought him back to his faith. (Imagine that! Words from a Mennonite writer brought a wandering Catholic man to faith.) This man started a men's ministry and invited me to his area to do several programs. I've now stayed at his home twice, and when I think about the love of Jesus I see pouring from that man, it brings me to tears.

Yes, my dear reader, I weep as I write this. I weep because I realize what God can do with average people who are obedient. I weep when I realize the power of words to change lives. I weep when I reflect on what Jesus did for me on the cross.

Did you know that *Hiking Through* was not even the book I intended to write when I first started out on the A.T.?

I wanted my obituary to be exciting reading. I wanted it to say that Mr. Stutzman left his job to thru-hike the Appalachian Trail and wrote a book about the adventure. The book I'd always dreamed about writing was either going to be about my hiking adventure or a collection of stories reflecting on life in general. That was the book I always thought I'd write.

But as I hiked northward toward Maine, God hiked along with me. I was a reluctant and slowly-emerging Enoch; I had invited God along on my hike, but my primary reason might have been so that I could talk to Him and keep firing my questions and laments toward Him. Nevertheless, as we hiked together, I began to hear God's thoughts.

One peaceful morning as I trekked up a steep hillside, nature worshipped all around me. A small brook flowed alongside the trail, whispering soothing sounds. Ahead of me, I saw a tree on which the leaves of one branch were dancing in the breeze. That branch alone shook and gyrated with joy while the other branches watched in wonderment.

I again asked my hiking partner a question I'd asked Him a dozen times before. "Where were You when Mary died? Were You there the night when she left us?"

Yes, Paul, I was there. Much like that butterfly following the light to freedom that night in your house, Mary followed the light and I brought her home. She is fine. Better than fine. But I want to talk with you about my plan for you.

"Plan? What plan?"

The book you're writing. I'm going to give you a message of hope to include in the book.

He told me what He wanted me to include. But I wasn't so sure about writing this message of *His* thoughts in *my* book. I voiced my objections and excuses.

"But why me? That message is for pastors to preach, not someone who's never written a book before and who is just a restaurant manager."

By yourself, you are no more than a restaurant manager. With me, you're a force.

"So You're telling me there was a purpose in bringing me out here?"

The book you're going to write will reach people pastors can't reach.

I confess, I still had my doubts.

"I'm not sure anyone will want to buy that book."

I'll put it into the hands of those who need to read it.

Had any other hiker come along that morning, they would have happened upon a hiker lying face-down on the trail, shedding many tears. But I arose from that position agreeing to do what God asked me to do.

I honestly can't say why God chose me to use in this way, but I know that *Hiking Through* has resonated with many people. Many who have suffered a great loss have been comforted by the message of hope. Some have returned to faith, and others have found the courage to step out in faith and obedience to something God is asking them to do.

In your life, you can write the book you always planned to write, or you can write a book you can't imagine. You can take a journey you have planned out in detail—which leaves little room for a close walk with God—or you can take courage and have faith and follow your Guide. He's looking for hearts that are courageous enough to follow Him.

I weep as I write this because I am so grateful my hiking partner convinced me that day to let Him be my guide. I am so glad I had the courage to do it. I can't say that I have always shown that courage. There have been times when I've held back, reasoned, rationalized, planned my own way, and generally gave Him excuses. But that day, I made a promise to Him. I kept my promise, and the journey has been something I never imagined.

Don't wait too long to abandon your own plans and ask God to guide you. He will take you to places you can't begin to imagine. You may even accomplish the impossible.

59

Plowing Straight

If you've decided to follow Enoch's example and walk with God, listening to His thoughts and following His Guide, then Jesus has a word you need to hear. His advice comes from a farming scenario.

I remember walking as a lad behind my grandfather as he plowed a field. He was an Amish farmer, with his hands on a plow pulled by a horse. Occasionally, the plow hit a stone and twisted, wrestling the plow handle from Grandfather's hand. He'd pick up the stone and carry it to the side of the field where he placed it on a pile of rocks he had removed over the years.

At a certain spot in the field, he skipped a small section and left it unplowed.

"Grandpa, why are you skipping that section?"

"It's for erosion control. When it rains, the water follows the contour of the field, and when I do not plow there, the grass will keep the field from eroding." I had never heard that word *erosion* before, and at that young age, I wasn't sure what he meant.

One thing I did know was that Grandfather did not look back as he plowed. Had he done so, he wouldn't have known where to stop plowing and his lines would have been crooked.

In Luke 9, Jesus makes an interesting statement about not looking back while plowing.

Jesus was on His way to Jerusalem. We have a glimpse here of what life was like on the road with Jesus. He had sent an advance team ahead to a Samaritan village where He wished to spend the night, but the villagers did not welcome Him. "Stay elsewhere," was the message received.

James and John took offense to this lack of hospitality. "Jesus," they suggested, "shall we call fire down from Heaven and obliterate that village?"

"No, let's go to another village instead."

Folks were still expressing a desire to become followers of Jesus. Luke recounts three such encounters. As Jesus and His disciples walked along, a man came up to Jesus and declared his intention to follow Jesus wherever He went. Jesus' reply was a caution: "Hospitality is sketchy. I often don't know where I'll sleep from one night to the next."

We don't know the man's response, but we do hear the excuses of the next fellow who showed up. Jesus invited this man to follow Him. This candidate could not leave home until he buried his dad. I imagine he meant he needed to take care of his parents until their demise. A third man signed up, but first he needed to go home to discuss it with family.

Jesus had heard enough excuses. He made a rather unusual statement in the last verse of Luke 9: "No one who puts his hands on the plow and looks back is fit for service in the kingdom of God."

Not fit to serve God? What could that mean?

I believe Jesus was speaking of commitment and being focused on a goal. He wanted disciples who were intentional about moving forward. In Paul's letter to the Philippians, Paul wrote about moving forward. He said there was one thing to do—forget about what's behind and strain toward the goal.

Once you've put your hand to the plow, you can't look back. Look ahead toward the goal. *Strain* toward the goal. Forget about what's behind. If you're looking back while intending to go ahead, your furrows will be crooked.

Plow straight, my friend.

60

Distractions

On our pilgrimage to our eternities, we all face numerous distractions. We're distracted when we lose our focus on what's most important in life. Distractions can be anything that prevents us from keeping our full attention where our attention should be.

We worry about things we can't possibly control. We worry about insignificant, trivial matters and miss the one thing needed.

One thing needed?

That's what Jesus told Martha one day.

Jesus had arrived at a village where two sisters invited Him in. Ironically, Luke 10 mentions it was Martha who opened their house to Him. However, Martha missed the opportunity of a lifetime when she let herself be distracted.

Martha was hustling about, making preparations for Jesus' stay. Meanwhile, her sister, Mary, was at Jesus' side, listening to the Teacher. Martha whined to Jesus about having to do all the work. "Tell Mary to come help me."

"Martha, Martha." Jesus said her name twice to emphasize just how important a message she was about to receive. "You've got yourself all worked up and upset about so many things. There is a better way, and your sister has chosen it."

Jesus does not say Martha was wrong in what she was doing, just that there was a better way. Her distractions prohibited her from seeing that better way.

"Only one thing is needed," said Jesus.

That one thing that Martha needed—and Mary chose—is the same one thing necessary for us today.

We need to listen to the Teacher.

The great distractor in our lives is the devil. He distracts us in cunning ways, keeping us from seeking the Teacher. He's adept at using unique strategies of distraction for each one of us, depending on our individual weaknesses and inclinations.

Psalm 25 is a good chapter on distractions. In this chapter, we can also learn how to avoid them.

David had become distracted. He writes that only the Lord could release his feet from the snare. My friend King David got snared so often. Yet God loved him. That always gives me such hope.

Turn to me and be gracious to me, for I am lonely and afflicted.

Loneliness can be such a distraction. "Poor, lonely me." However, loneliness should drive you straight to the Teacher. Take your lonely self to a lonely place and pray.

The troubles of my heart have multiplied, free me from my anguish. Look upon my affliction and my distress.

Wow, my buddy David was in a bad way. He had allowed himself to be so distracted from the plans God had for him, and now we can see the cumulative results of his distractions.

David begs God to take away all his sins. There's the crux of the matter. His distractions had led him into sin.

Have distractions kept you from the Teacher?

Have distractions led you into sin?

Are you secretly looking at sites on your computer you would be embarrassed for your spouse or children to see? Are you watching or reading material that grieves the Holy Spirit and fouls His temple? How about this one: Have you filled your schedule so full of "good and respectable" activity (yes, even church activities) that you can't find time to sit with the Teacher?

Go to the Teacher and make the request David did in Psalm 25.

Show me your ways, Lord, teach me your paths. Guide me in your truth and teach me, for you are God my Savior, and my hope is in you all day long.

That broad road leading to destruction has all varieties of attractive distractions. Distractions along that road are necessary. The devil certainly can't have those folks reminded of where that road ends.

The narrow path is where the Teacher walks and teaches. It offers so much more than the distracted road. It offers peace and contentment.

Join me there.

Don't wait too long!

61

From Strength to Strength

My uncle Roman was a pastor at a local church. I often heard him refer to the pilgrimage of Psalm 84 and speak of the Valley of Baka. This psalm may be set in a different time and place, but it lays out truths from God that we can all experience. Little did I know how many pilgrimages my own life would travel and that the Valley of Baka exists in my world and my day.

Psalms 84 is a song about pilgrimage. The 2,176-mile Appalachian Trail hike was a pilgrimage toward a goal of finding healing after the death of my wife. On the Camino and my hike through Israel, I was looking for more answers to questions I had about following Jesus. Every one of my "adventures" was a pilgrimage of sorts; and even the adventure of everyday living, when I may not have walked more than a mile from home, has been a pilgrimage.

In Psalm 84, the writer speaks about going from strength to strength. On the AT pilgrimage, I went from strength to weakness to exhaustion. Do your days or weeks ever follow that progression?

David is believed to be the writer of this psalm. He speaks of going on pilgrimage to Zion, to the temple of the living God, where he longs to enter the courtyard and be near God. He remembers sparrows and swallows nesting in the temple and thinks how fortunate they are to have their homes and raise their young so near to the altar of the Lord God Almighty. David would have been familiar with the design of the temple and could visualize these sparrows and swallows living in the presence of God.

This pilgrimage to the temple was made with families and friends traveling together. Undoubtedly, there were songs sung, and I'm certain at times laughter rang out as the crowd progressed. However, there were also times of sadness, much like our own pilgrimages.

Before reaching Jerusalem, the pilgrimage route traversed a dry, barren valley. The Valley of Baka, also called the Valley of Weeping, was a place where you would expect joy to be at the lowest levels. But because of the pilgrims' great hope and their gladness at coming near to the living God, they made this barren valley "a place of springs."

This pathway we're following, this "way everlasting," leads us home to our Father and Creator. We walk in anticipation of being with Him, in the homes He's prepared for us. Our God will live with His people!

But we go through barren valleys. We trudge along where the road is hard, the environment harsh, and the elements all seem to be working against us. Perhaps pilgrims to Jerusalem knew where this valley lay and they could prepare for the grueling walk through it. But in our pilgrimages, we usually stumble into this valley unwarned and unprepared.

My uncle loved to encourage us, reminding us that whenever we go through our own Valley of Baka, we have the power within us to turn the valley into springs of living water. The power within us is the Spirit of God Himself. Our strength comes from Him. And it flows outward to other pilgrims. Uncle Roman liked to say that if we find strength in the midst of these valleys, we can be a type of pilgrim oasis where other folks can find respite. We become wells of living water for other hurting pilgrims on their own pilgrimage, traveling from strength to strength.

A proverb from the wise King Solomon reminds us: "Those who refresh others will themselves be refreshed," and the traditional King James uses the same metaphor of water and springs we have been using here: "And he that watereth shall be watered also himself" (Proverbs 11:25).

The final verse in Psalm 84 reminds us that those who trust in the Lord will be blessed. Whether you are looking for strength to get through the Valley of Weeping or you are sharing your strength with others, be blessed and refreshed, Pilgrim!

62

The Big Picture

In the church of my youth, we were required to follow some strict rules. I chafed under what I believed was a bit of oppression. All right, then—I did think it was a lot of oppression. At times, after a particularly stringent message on Sunday morning, I would question my father about the restrictions placed upon us.

"Son, you need to see the big picture," he would say.

Apparently, there was a small picture and a big one. I must have been viewing the small pictures. I did enjoy art and recognized picture size quickly: small, medium, and large. And then there was big. I wasn't certain if the big picture came before or after the large one.

As I grew older and a bit wiser, I did grasp the meaning of Dad's advice.

Recently, I had the privilege of visiting the Getty Museum in Los Angeles, California. I've found that I enjoy art museums. A visit is not only pleasurable, it also enhances my writing. I sometimes suffer brain blockage and can't write with passion. The words are stuck in a cluster in my brain cells. A trip to an art museum unblocks them. There is something freeing about viewing and interpreting art. My interpretation of what the artist is trying to convey isn't always what the artist intended, but that's the beauty of art. Anyone can take away whatever that piece of art speaks to them.

Art stimulates my brain and the word cluster is freed.

One of my daughters lives in Philadelphia, Pennsylvania. In that city is an amazing museum called the Barnes Foundation; I found it to be an art lover's paradise. Many art museums consider themselves fortunate to offer a few masterpieces from artists such as Cézanne or Renoir. The Barnes Foundation overwhelms me with its quality and quantity. They have 181 Renoirs, 59 Matisses, and 69 Cézannes. The entire collection is valued in excess of 25 billion dollars.

Several years ago, I was able to fulfill a dream of visiting a world-famous art museum, the Louvre, in Paris, France. I was en route to the south of France, where I planned to hike a trail known as the Camino de Santiago. (*Camino* means *path*, or *way*.) I intended to walk over the Pyrenees mountain range in southern France and then through the entirety of northern Spain. The official trail ends in Santiago, Spain.

I flew into Paris and planned to take the train to Saint-Jean-Pied-de-Port, a little town located in the foothills of the Pyrenees. The French section of the Camino starts in this town.

Once in Paris, I had a day before my departure, so I took the opportunity to visit the Louvre Museum. The most famous painting in the world resides in this museum. The *Mona Lisa*, by Leonardo da Vinci, is known as the most visited art object in the world. One needs to fight masses of humanity to get close to the portrait.

When I viewed it for the first time, I felt a brief adrenalin rush. *I'm seeing the famous Mona Lisa!* This was followed almost immediately by *Wow, that's so little.* Let's just say the Mona Lisa represents the little-picture category of pictures. The size of this painting is 30 inches by 21 inches. It's called a half-length portrait. Very soon, my thoughts progressed to, *What's the big deal about her? There are so many bigger and more interesting pieces of art. And some of them actually give you the whole, big picture.*

That day in the Louvre, Dad's advice to see the big picture took on more meaning.

With any painting, whether in a museum or hanging in my own home, I enjoy standing close enough to examine the small details the artist has included. Why are those details there? How does each relate to the rest of the picture? After analyzing small details, I step back to view the big picture.

Often, the big picture shows me clearly why the small details were necessary.

In relation to Dad's advice about the church, seeing the big picture meant I needed to take the small detail I didn't understand and view it in the context of the big picture the pastors wanted to keep in focus for us. They believed guardrails needed to be installed to keep church members on the straight and narrow pathway. They were the artists in our church life, and that put the paint brush in their hands to paint details they believed were essential to the big picture.

Our lives are a lot like a painting.

What would folks think if they looked closely at the little individual details of your life? Were you to look at my painting, I'm certain you would see details that would give you cause for pause. Your thoughts might be along these lines: *You did that? You went there? I wouldn't have thought you capable of that.*

But wait, you're not seeing the big picture.

Step back, and take a look at the entirety of my life so far.

Do you see where those troubling details are that gave you pause? Do you see the cross painted there? Those troubling details are scattered around the base of the cross.

Look beyond the cross. Don't you see how the scene shifts?

Up close, it all looks a bit messy. Step back to see the big picture, and you'll have an entirely different perspective.

It almost looks like two artists worked on my painting, doesn't it?

It's true. There have been two different artists.

I made a choice one day and handed my paintbrush to Jesus. His hand now applies those bright splashes of blue, red, green, and yellow as he paints the adventures of life following Him.

Do you want the painting of your life turned into a masterpiece? Hand that paintbrush over to the greatest artist ever. Your painting won't be a half portrait like the most famous painting in the world. Your portrait will be a full portrait, showing you with brilliant splashes of love, joy, and peace. Sure, there will be some dark valleys mixed in as well. But there are glorious mountaintop vistas, too.

Step back, take a look at your big picture thus far. Are you sad about the mess you've created, or is the cross visible, painted over your life in bold red?

If not, hand that brush over and really start living.

Don't wait too long.

63

Parable of the Lost Key

In Luke chapter 15, Jesus tells a group of tax collectors and sinners three parables about things that were lost. The three were a sheep, a lost coin, and a lost son.

All three might have remained lost forever. The sheep that had wandered away certainly could have met a wild animal on the prowl and come to an untimely end. The lost coin could have been picked up and claimed by someone else. The prodigal son's father could reasonably believe he might never see his son again.

However, in all three instances, the lost was found, and great rejoicing followed.

Several years ago, I suffered a loss. As losses go, it didn't rise to the level of the loss of a relationship. The situation did, however, cost me money to replace what was lost.

What bothered me the most was that I had lost this item. I rarely lose anything. I have a place for everything. The place for this item was in my left pants pocket. It always occupied a place at the bottom of the pocket and shared the space with my cell phone.

For years, my cell phone and my post office key had resided side by side in sweet accord in my pocket.

One day, only my cell phone resided there.

I searched everywhere. Perhaps I had left it stuck in my box at the post office. Not there. I inquired at the counter: Had anyone turned in a lost key? No, no one. I searched my car numerous times. Between the seats and under the seats. Not one square inch of that car was unexamined. I even followed the example of the lady who had lost the coin in Jesus' parable. I lit my lamps and swept my house, seeking that lost key.

However, it was not found and there was no rejoicing. Close to two years later, I was still lamenting the loss—and the cost of a replacement key.

How was it possible to lose a key that was always in that pocket? Granted, it could have gone through my washing machine. I will admit to washing my wallet twice in the years since my wife passed away. But laundered money wasn't the key to what had happened.

I take long hikes on a local biking and hiking trail. It's where I go for thoughts—God thoughts and relaxing thoughts about life and nature. The trail is shared by hundreds of bicycles, walkers, runners, and horses and buggies. (I'm in Amish Country. You won't find many trails in America where Amish buggies drive alongside runners and bikers.) The trail wanders through trees, fields, and swamps. Lots of swamps.

One day, I had walked about two miles on this trail and had just turned around for the two-mile trek back. For some unknown reason, I paused to look at nature around me. On both sides of the trail lay swamps. I glanced down at the pavement—again, for reasons unknown.

Directly beneath me, an inch away from my shoe, lay a key.

It looked just like a post office key, except the normal brass coloration was blackened. The key blended so well with the blacktop trail that the only way a person could see it was to be directly over it.

I wondered if someone from the neighboring town might have dropped it. I determined to take it to the local post office and turn it in. At least, if I couldn't find mine, I could make someone else happy by returning their key. They could commence with inviting their neighbors and rejoicing together at finding their lost item.

When I returned home that day, I took the key I'd found out of my pocket. It reminded me again of my own loss. On a whim, I wanted to see how similar the keys were. I held the found key against the key I had purchased to replace the lost one. They seemed to be a perfect match.

It's surely not possible, I thought.

Nevertheless, I took it along the next morning and inserted it into the lock on my mailbox. It inserted easily. I was shocked when I turned the key and it opened my mailbox.

How was that even possible? Yet it was. It was my missing key.

Several days later, I was again walking that same trail when a trail maintenance vehicle approached. A powerful blower attached to the tractor was blowing leaves and other detritus off the trail.

I flagged down the driver and asked if he would like to hear my story about finding my lost key on the trail after two years. He was in disbelief as I recalled how I had lost it so long ago and then found it again. He told me he plowed the snow off the trail in winter and used the blower twice a month. My key should have been blown or scraped into the swamp a long time ago.

But it wasn't. And it was found.

Apparently, I received a phone call that day several years ago, and when I pulled the phone from my pocket the key came along for the ride and dropped to the ground. I tested my theory by returning the key to my pocket with the cell phone. The next time my phone rang, I pulled it out and answered it. My key had been sequestered at the bottom of my phone case and it dropped to the trail.

How it remained at that spot for all that time over winters and summers while runners, walkers, bicycles, and horses ran over it is a mystery. How it defied snow plows and blowers and stayed where it fell awaiting my return, is inexplicable.

The key now resides in the console of my vehicle.

Jesus often told parables the disciples didn't understand. He had to spell out the truths in simpler terms. I questioned God, too. I wanted an explanation. *What are you teaching me through this parable of the lost key?*

Perhaps Jesus was reminding me that folks in our lives who seem lost and unreachable really aren't. Like the prodigal son, who was still loved and watched for by his father, everyone is loved and watched for by the heavenly Father. He wants the lost found.

And perhaps God was just showing me He can do the impossible—with ease.

64

Poured Out

My wife loved Niagara Falls. I love it as well, and for a good reason: We spent our honeymoon there many years ago.

Mary's favorite spot to stand and watch the falls was directly over the rim, where the water cascaded downward. She was mesmerized by the movement of the water as it took the plunge to the swirling pools below.

When I set out to pedal my bicycle around the five Great Lakes, I decided to make Lake Ontario the first of the five. At 3:00 AM one morning, I loaded my bicycle in my car and headed for Niagara Falls. I wanted to start my ride at the identical spot by the falls where we had so often stood.

By 8:00 AM, my bicycle and I were at Mary's favorite spot. The thundering cascade of water created a mist that swirled all around me. I thought about all the water that has plunged over that spot at Niagara Falls since those carefree days in May so long ago and the many tears that have flowed down my face since those days. The memories of days of unbridled joy created more tears, which flowed freely as well. I realized something that day. I admitted that I no longer enjoyed doing these adventures alone. Spots like Niagara Falls are for people in love, not for folks alone.

Something in that flowing water of Niagara was soothing and spoke to Mary's soul. What was it? I never asked. I just know that I loved standing beside her as the tumbling water filled her with joy.

I enjoy flowing water, too. Every morning I step into the shower, and water falls over me. That awakens me and is soon followed by a cup of coffee. Both my insides and my outsides are now awake, ready for more water. My preparations for the day are complete when I've also stood under the cascading flow of spiritual water. Body and soul are then prepared to be led. Then I am the David of Psalm 23: *He leads me beside still waters. He restores my soul.*

Psalm 23 is a comforting passage. It speaks of contentment, rest, and peace. But that's not always a description of us, is it? Perhaps Psalm 22 more accurately describes you right now.

The difference between Psalm 22 and Psalm 23 is jarring. Psalm 22 opens with David's cry, "My God, my God, why have you forsaken me?" Chapter 23 opens with: "The LORD is my shepherd, I shall not want."

Quite a contrast.

In Psalm 22, David feels as though God has forsaken him. In deep distress, he cries out to God but doesn't seem to get answers. He remembers that his ancestors trusted God and were delivered, but David is low in spirit. As low as a worm. He even says, "I am a worm, and not a man."

Fortunately for David and myself, there are different kinds of worms. Had he been a regular earthworm, he could have been dangling from a fish hook. However, David and I were caterpillar worms, with butterfly potential. It was just a matter of time.

He goes on with his lamentations. He's surrounded by bulls seeking to stomp him to death and lions intent on tearing him apart. He gives up completely; he has exhausted all his own resources, and there is no one to revive or help him.

He says, "I am poured out like water" (Psalm 22:14). He is done. He has nothing more left. He is totally drained, depleted, sapped, and spent. He is empty.

Eight days after I biked away from Niagara Falls, I returned to the same location, completing my bicycle ride around Lake Ontario. As I stood at Mary's spot, my tears flowed again as I recalled all those fond memories of love so long ago. My tears dripped over the edge and joined the thundering water pouring onto the sacrificial rocks below. The rising mist covered my face and returned my tears.

I felt like David in Psalm 22 when he wrote, "I am poured out like water."

I was empty, exhausted, with nothing of myself left.

Have you been there, too?

Paul uses a similar phrase in Philippians 2:17: "But even if I am being poured out like a drink offering..." He is in jail at the time he writes this, and he's aware that he will die.

Paul is also being poured out, but this pouring is different; he's added a phase—"like a drink offering." This completely changes the picture of being emptied and spent.

You'll remember that God gave detailed instructions to Moses and the Israelites for many types of sacrifices to be made at different times and for different situations. A drink offering was always accompanied by another offering, possibly a bird or a lamb. Wine or water was poured on top of this offering. The water or wine poured out on top of the already-burning sacrifice turned into a mist and mixed with the smoke, creating a sweet-smelling sacrifice to God.

The drink offering represented giving oneself wholly to God, a total giving up of self.

Paul was beheaded. His blood was poured out. It was poured out on the sacrifice of the faith the Philippians had made. His life had been poured out for God's work, and his life-blood was poured out for his faith.

Can we offer such a sacrifice to God?

One of my favorite drink-offering stories from the Bible again involves King David. The account is found in 1 Chronicles 11:16.

Saul had just taken his own life. He died because he had been unfaithful to the Lord. The elders of Israel came to David, who was still hiding out from Saul. They wanted David to be king, since Saul was dead.

David accepted and immediately determined to recapture Jerusalem, which had been taken over by the Jebusites. David defeated them, took up residence in the city, and rebuilt it. Jerusalem became known as "the city of David."

David had a force of incredible men around him. They were the best warriors in all the land. Thirty of them were known as David's "mighty men."

Three of this top thirty were with David one day when he was in an introspective mood. I imagine him reflecting back on his life as a shepherd boy, tending sheep in and around Bethlehem. A spring near the gate of Bethlehem gushed with water that David loved. On hot days, watching his father's sheep, he would become very thirsty.

You surely know how that is on a hot day, when you're so thirsty that no beverage but cold water will slake your thirst.

My grandmother had a spring in the corner of her basement. The water there has flowed continually for over 150 years. My grandmother stored fruit and vegetables in a trench holding the cold spring water. It served as a refrigerator. On really hot days, I'd be out in the field with other workers, making hay or shocking wheat. Our throats would get dry and parched, and we would stomp down those steps to the corner spring. A granite cup always hung from a nail. We took turns dipping the cup into the spring and drinking deeply from the sweet, life-sustaining water.

Years later, there were times I'd be passing my grandmother's farm and I would long for water from that spring. I'd stop and head to that basement corner where I would drink not only the cool, sweet water but also the sweet memories. Often, my grandmother wouldn't even know I had visited her corner spring.

That's why David's statement that day makes sense to me. I can feel his thirst for water from the spring that brought back memories for him. He expressed his longing to his three mighty men. "Oh, that someone would get me a drink of water from the well near the gate of Bethlehem."

Now, Bethlehem is only about five miles from Jerusalem, but there was one major problem. A band of Philistines (David's long-time enemies) were camped outside of the town, making access to this well impossible.

That is, impossible for most people.

But David's three mighty men were known for their fearlessness and fierceness in battle. In addition, these men loved and honored David so much they risked their lives and burst through the Philistines' lines.

They brought back the drink of water David so longed for.

And then comes the twist: David was so moved by their allegiance to him that he refused to drink it! He poured out the water before the Lord as a drink offering to his mighty men.

Let's go back to Psalms 22. This psalm also foretells Jesus' suffering on the cross for us. He poured Himself out for all mankind. He made Himself nothing, so we could become everything.

Ephesians 5:2 says Christ "gave himself up for us as a fragrant offering and sacrifice to God," because He loved us. In the same verse, Paul says we should also live a life of love, following Christ's example.

Am I willing to be poured out like a drink offering, bringing such a fragrant offering to the Lord? Do I love that much?

The Birthday Story

You remember I mentioned my plan to come to Jesus once all the excitement of my earthly life was fading away. Fortunately for me, my brain did develop better reasoning. How did wiser thoughts become more frequent visitors in my head? Punishment. That might seem odd, but allow me to explain.

There were times I was naughty. (You seem surprised!) Yes, I was spanked.

Spankings didn't do much good, though, other than to burn up some calories for dear Dad. He tried a new approach. He made me read the Bible. Yes, he punished me by making me read the Bible. Some might say that's the wrong approach to both Bible reading and punishment, that children will never want to read Scripture if it is forced on them.

My dad was kind. He was wise. He knew what was best for his son.

Haven't we all come to Dad and begged and pleaded for something? I sure did that. The answer wasn't always to my liking, but my wise dad knew what I needed.

All my friends had BB guns. It's possible that my perception was a bit askew; perhaps not every one of them had a gun, but it sure seemed that way to me. I begged and pleaded with Dad for a Daisy BB gun for my birthday. I even showed him the picture in the Sears & Roebuck catalog. It was a $24 thing of beauty. That was a lot of money for Dad back in the late Fifties. But I was his son, and surely he wanted what was best for his only son.

My birthday arrived. I greeted the day with great anticipation. I had prayed fervently for that gun and fully expected my prayer to be answered.

However, the wrapped gift Dad gave me that day was way too small to hold the treasured BB gun. Perhaps it just held the BBs, and the larger package was yet to come.

Somewhat dejectedly, I opened up the gift and...

Nooooooooo!

Inside was a Bible.

I was devastated. What was Dad thinking? Perhaps he thought I'd shoot my eye out.

In Dad's wisdom, he gifted me with something far more powerful than any gun. Dad knew what the better gift was. He knew a BB gun could make me happy for a season, but he also knew a Bible could make me a better person for a lifetime and prepare me for an eternity after this lifetime.

That was the Bible Dad made me read when I was bad. (I've always thought I was a good kid, but now as I reflect upon those days, I did read that Bible a lot.)

Instead of spankings, Dad made me read Psalms and Proverbs. I sometimes look back and wonder why I didn't just pretend to read it. But I was an honorable naughty kid. I obeyed and read both books. And Proverbs changed my life.

When I read about Solomon asking for wisdom, I determined to do the same myself. Perhaps I believed I'd get wealthy like Solomon. I certainly didn't believe for the number of wives he had. That's frowned upon here in Amish Country.

That "punishment" and its resultant wisdom-seeking was over sixty years ago. I still pray for wisdom every day. I'm still a work in progress. God gives me wisdom in small doses. Sometimes wisdom arrives even before *Amen,* and sometimes it arrives immediately after doing something really stupid. (You understand that, don't you?) Wisdom has also protected me, keeping me from foolish choices.

It's an ongoing process, a lifetime journey, accumulating priceless wisdom along the way. God's promised to walk the entire journey with me, and I'm confident He'll fulfill His promises.

Active Wisdom

Jesus had just chosen the twelve disciples and had given them their marching orders. He had begun teaching and preaching in areas around Galilee when several messengers approached Him.

"We've been sent by John the Baptist to find out if you're the one he's been prophesying about," they told Jesus.

He told them to go back to the prison where John was being held and report on what they had witnessed: blind people got their sight back, the lame walked, the deaf heard, and dead folks had come back to life.

"The folks who do not doubt Me will be blessed," Jesus emphasized.

As John's disciples were leaving, Jesus turned to the crowd to talk about His cousin John.

"When you folks went out to the wilderness to hear John, what did you expect him to be like? Did you think he'd be like grass, just blowing in the breeze, or some dressed-up prince? No, he is a prophet. Not just any prophet, though. He is the prophet who was chosen by God to prepare the way for my arrival. My cousin John is the greatest person ever born to a woman. That is, he was the greatest person born under the old covenant, the law."

Then Jesus added an astonishing statement: "But even the least person in the Kingdom of Heaven is greater than John the Baptist."

Imagine that. If you are a follower of Jesus, if God the Father has moved you from the kingdom of darkness to the kingdom of His Son, you are counted as being greater than John the Baptist. That should make you feel very special. C.H. Spurgeon once wrote, "The least in the gospel stands on higher ground than the greatest under the law." Greater than Moses? Abraham? Elijah? Are you realizing just how fortunate we are to be living on this side of the law?

Those living in this Kingdom can walk with God, communicate with Him through the Holy Spirit, and hear His wise God-thoughts. I love those walks. Most of this book was written after walks like that. I sometimes wonder why everyone doesn't thirst for these walks.

As Jesus preached about the Kingdom of Heaven coming, He encountered both belief and rejection. In Matthew 11, He denounced cities in which He had preached but had found no repentance. You would think that after all the miracles He performed, these folks would want to become converts. You'd think they would want to know this God and His thoughts. However, many rejected both John's preaching and Jesus' message.

They were like many folks today. Nothing pleases them. They miss miracles happening all around them and wonder why they don't have joy. Folks with critical hearts will always find something which will make them unhappy. Jesus compared them to little children who couldn't be pleased.

When they should have been happy hearing flute music, they weren't. When sad songs were sung at a funeral, they didn't mourn. It seems like a cantankerous bunch of people. They even criticized John for his strange diet and refusal to drink wine, then disapproved of Jesus when He did enjoy a good meal.

"He hangs out with tax collectors, and yes, even sinners. He eats and drinks with them. He's a glutton and a drunkard." Wow! That's quite a disparagement of the One sent to save you!

There were folks who did believe in the message John delivered, and they were thrilled to know that the Messiah had finally come. In their eagerness to get to know Him, they walked long distances and sat all day to hear Him teach. To those, Jesus said, "But wisdom is proved right by her actions" (Matthew 11:19).

Are you wise?

Active wisdom is a father giving a son a Bible instead of a BB gun.

Active wisdom is a disappointed son actually reading that Bible.

Active wisdom is being a good example to your children.

Active wisdom is honoring your spouse.

Active wisdom is truthful.

Active wisdom is honest.

Be wise. Put your wisdom in action.

Don't wait too long. That wouldn't be wise!

Words Have Meaning

On an April morning, my two hiking buddies and I were about to ascend the heights of the Smoky Mountains. We had just left Fontana Village that morning, blessed with a blue sky overhead. Good food and a good night's rest had prepared us for the day's upward trek. A steep climb awaited us as we left the village, loaded down with a week's supply of food. We hoped to get on top of "Old Smoky" and traverse many miles that day.

Ahead, a park sign posted trail maps and other bits of information and trail advice. A fresh notice had been posted. "Hiker Advisory," read the headline. The notice warned hikers about a predicted storm approaching the Smokies. We were to consider carefully our hiking plans for the day.

"It's a hiker advisory, but it doesn't tell us what to do," was my flippant remark.

"Words have meaning," replied my hiking buddy.

How true. Words have the power to cause deep emotional hurts. Words also have healing power.

I recall a day in Salisbury, Connecticut, a stop on my Appalachian Trail hike.

My buddy Fargo and I hiked nearly twenty-two miles that day. My guidebook showed several lodging opportunities in Salisbury. One was a house owned by an eighty-one-year-old widow. For $35 a person, we would have a comfortable bed and a shower available to us.

We were still several miles from town when I called her.

"Hello, Maria, there are two mid-fifties, good-looking men wanting to stay at your house tonight," I said.

"I will pick you up where the trail crosses Lower Coble Road," she replied. "But first, I have to finish a card game I'm playing with a friend. If I'm not there, wait for me."

She was there, standing on the trail. As we approached, she yelled at us, "I was promised good-looking men!"

"Give us time to shower the trail off us, and you'll be impressed how we look and smell," we replied.

Later that evening, we were chatting with Maria at her kitchen table. She removed a notebook from a nearby shelf and pushed it across to me.

"What's this?"

"People write about their experience staying with me," she replied. Then she made a remark I'll never forget. "In the cold of winter when I'm lonely, I read from this notebook. I read the nice things people have written about me, and it comforts me."

Yes, folks, words do have meaning.

Back to the day of the hiker advisory and our climb up into the Smoky Mountains. We did confirm the words to the old song "On Top of Old Smoky." It was covered in snow. The words of that song speak of someone losing their true love for courting too slow: a possible harbinger of things to come in my future courtship of a lovely lady.

The storm started out as small pellets of snow bouncing off a field of small white wildflowers. It was a beautiful sight—until the weather turned nasty. Wind and blowing snow greeted us as we approached the heights of the mountain.

A forest ranger met us and advised us to get into the first shelter possible to wait out the storm. We hiked only thirteen miles that day and shortly after noon reached Mollies Ridge Shelter. That afternoon and night, thirty people crammed into a twelve-person shelter.

Outside, the storm raged. My hiking buddy looked at me and said, "Words have meaning."

Are there words you have spoken you wish you had back? Have you hurt others with painful cutting words? I have. I've also had words used against me that hurt deeply. Words have healed me, too. I've used words to forgive, and I've used words to ask for forgiveness.

On this path we're walking with our Guide, our words can be powerful. Perhaps you are the one—and the only one—who has the right words to heal a hurting person.

Or do you need to ask for forgiveness from someone you have hurt?

Do it now! Don't wait too long.

68

Delightful, Delicious, Protective Words

Jeremiah was called by God to warn Judah about their wickedness. He was often in danger, targeted by religious and political leaders who were upset about the message he delivered.

In Jeremiah 15, we see the prophet reminding God how he had suffered at the hands of his persecutors. He longed to hear from God. In verse 16 he does hear from God, and here is his response: "When your words came, I devoured them, they were my joy and my heart's delight."

He ate those words like life-giving food.

If you've invited the Spirit of God into your life, you, too, will be able to feast on these words from God. No calorie-laden food can do what these words will do for you.

Is your spiritual tank low? Are you hungry for words of encouragement? Do you need a reminder that God loves you? Are you tired of being sad and lonely?

Does it seem like you're alone on your journey through life? You are not alone. The Spirit of God walks with you, to comfort, advise, teach, and help. He'll feed you, too. Ask Him, then open your Bible.

Those nourishing words from a loving God will give you sustenance for your day.

Devouring God's words will also be your protection. Remember the monarch caterpillar. As soon as it hatches, it starts eating, eating, eating. Caterpillars can strip a milkweed plant of all its leaves. In that milkweed is a substance that repels birds that might otherwise eat the small caterpillars. Likewise, what we take in as we feast on God's Word is not only nourishment for growth but also protection against forces that seek to destroy *us*.

Follow the example of Jeremiah 15:16, and devour the words of God. It's best you don't actually ingest the actual pages, but eat those words. They will be to you like the milkweed to the butterflies. The truth you take in will make you repulsive to the devil as you metamorphose from a worm to a beautiful child of God. As the name of the butterfly suggests, you will become royalty yourself.

69

Sheep and Goats

May I ask: Are you a sheep or a goat?

When I was in the third grade, my teacher often talked about the two young goats he had when he was young. He told us stories about those kids jumping and playing and running all over their property. He loved those little goats. I begged my dad to buy me a goat as a pet. My begging produced the same results as my pleas for a BB gun. I did not get a goat.

Doesn't a "pet goat" seem more appealing than a "pet sheep"? Jesus used both in His teachings. I imagine that's because the critters were a familiar sight around Capernaum and Nazareth, and folks could understand the point He was making. The two animals are similar in some ways, but they do have many differing characteristics.

In Matthew 25: 31-46, Jesus draws sharp distinctions between sheep and goats. One is qualified for Heaven; the other is not.

You don't have to give me an answer to my opening question. Instead, look into the mirror in this section of

Scripture; you will see a reflection of the characteristics of your own life. Is there a sheep or a goat looking back at you?

Sheep are gentle and meek. They will follow a leader. Goats are more independent and are actually more intelligent than a sheep. Sheep eat grass. Goats will eat anything. In these characteristics, I must confess that I'm more goat than sheep.

However, what both these animals represent at the Day of Judgment is the focus of Matthew 25 and my thoughts now as I write.

Jesus had been teaching the disciples and crowds of people at the temple. In chapter 24, He left the temple and took a short walk to the Mount of Olives. This could have been one of those times when He was seeking some alone-time with His Father. The next verse does say that His disciples came to Him "privately."

They had questions. Jesus had made references to things that were going to happen in the future. The disciples wanted to know *When will these things happen? How will we know it's all happening?*

Jesus did inform them about some events that needed to occur first, but He told them no one but God knew the precise time.

He did, however, give them some details about who would be admitted to Heaven when that time did arrive. I'm sure some disciples remembered the Sermon on the Mount, when Jesus reminded them that not everyone who said, "Lord, Lord" would be admitted. "Only those who do the will of God." Many folks will say they prophesied and drove out demons and performed many miracles in Jesus' name. That does seem like good recommendations for those seeking admittance to Heaven. However, Jesus will tell them plainly, "I never knew you. Get away from me, you evildoers."

That's scary stuff there!

It would have been helpful if Jesus had told folks in Matthew 7 what the will of God was, rather than waiting until Matthew 25. Fortunately, since you're reading this, you will be given these qualifications. Yes, a chance to be transformed from a goat to a sheep.

Jesus described the scene: The nations will be gathered before Him. Like a shepherd separates his flock, Jesus will separate the sheep from the goats. The sheep go to the right side, the goats to the left.

Then Jesus will turn to the right and address the sheep. "Come on in. Get your inheritance. You are free to come in since you fed Me when I was hungry. You gave Me something to drink when I was thirsty. I needed a place to stay, and you invited Me in. I needed clothes; you gave Me clothes. You even visited Me in prison."

Something odd happens now. If I were a sheep person, I'd be making a run for the pearly gates. "I'm in!" However, the righteous are baffled. They want to know when they had seen Jesus in any of those conditions or had done any of those things He listed.

"Whenever you did any of those deeds for the least of humanity, you did it for Me," the Lord replies.

Jesus turns to the goats next. Chances are, they are wandering about, confident they will also be included. After all, didn't they prophesy, didn't they do miracles and cast out demons? I imagine they might be thinking they've been singled out for even greater rewards.

But they, too, are dumbfounded by Jesus words: "Goats, depart! You are cursed."

"But... why?"

"You didn't feed Me, give Me drink, clothe Me, or visit Me when I was sick and in prison."

"But Lord, we never saw You in those conditions."

Had the goats been paying attention, they would already have heard the answer. It was the same answer the sheep had been given.

We tend to make following Jesus harder than it is. Sheep willingly follow their Shepherd. Perhaps that's why Jesus used sheep and goats in illustrations. A shepherd seeks a lost sheep. When was the last time you heard of someone seeking a lost goat? I can almost visualize that parable. There was one goat in the goat fold. Ninety-nine had wandered away.

So, what's a goat to do?

Stop prophesying and start feeding people. Worry less about demons and prophecy, and clothe people, shelter people, visit the sick and imprisoned.

That will get you on the "right" side of Jesus.

Become a sheep.

70

The Least of These

Have you ever met one of those "least of these" folks Jesus was talking about?

Both the sheep and the goats had unknowingly met least-of-these people. And how they had treated such people is the differentiating factor for Jesus' separation of the sheep and goats.

Where have we met such people? Do we recognize them?

My training to be a sheep started with an encounter in my own church. Kyle is a young man with cerebral palsy. He had just started coming to our church when I first met him.

Our church has a time of open sharing. Anyone can speak, possibly requesting prayer or sharing some life-changing event that may have recently occurred.

A person with cerebral palsy often has severe speech difficulties, and Kyle was no exception. When he spoke, his arms flailed and he struggled to produce words that could be understood. What would take one minute for me to say, took Kyle five minutes to enunciate. Fortunately, our youth pastor spent enough time with Kyle that he could understand what

Kyle was trying to convey, and he would often "translate" what Kyle had just said. Impatient and thoughtless, I fidgeted in my seat and wondered why Kyle didn't just write what he wished to say and have the youth pastor read it to the congregation. That would get us to lunch five minutes sooner.

Okay, you're thinking I'm a terrible person. In reality, I was a bit shortsighted. God had a lesson to teach me about being a sheep in a world where the goats seem to make the rules of life.

Kyle wanted to be a writer. He wanted to write about life experiences from his point of view. Specifically, he wanted to write a book. That was a much-cherished goal. But he knew nothing about the book-writing process and had no idea even how to get started. He needed a sheep to assist him.

But where could he find such a sheep in the church? Was there someone in church who just may have written a book… or seven?

Calling all sheep! Sheep, wake up! Help needed!

Oh yes, that's me. I could help. I've helped numerous people in the book-writing business. But all the other people whose questions I'd answered and to whom I'd lent a hand were so much easier to understand. We'd had "normal" conversations.

I think I'll pass, thank you just the same.

One day, the youth pastor suggested to me that perhaps I could help Kyle.

Oh, youth pastor and Jesus, I can't.

"He wants to speak to you about it," said the youth pastor.

(I do have Kyle's permission to write this. If anyone should be hesitant to see the truth of this story in published form, it would be me, the goat in the fold.)

Kyle sat at the very front of the church. From there, the

pastor could easily see Kyle's expressions and flailings and understand what he was saying.

I'm a creature of habit. I sit in the same pew every Sunday, about five rows from the back and in the aisle seat. I'm an aisle person. I need a quick-and-easy exit plan. (Yes, I do back into parking spots.) With precision timing, I can be out of a building in seconds, if necessary.

I knew Kyle wanted to meet me after the service, but by the time he made it back to the foyer, I was a mile towards lunch.

That went on for a few weeks. Then he got wise to my tricks.

One Sunday, as we began the closing song, he stumbled his way back toward the foyer. And waited.

I was trapped.

"Good one, Kyle! You got me."

"I... want... to write... a... book. Can you... help... me?"

What could I say? I agreed to meet him the following week at a coffee shop in a nearby town. I doubt that any goat could have turned down the poor fellow. Perhaps I wasn't a goat, but just a reluctant sheep.

We did meet. I purchased a donut and coffee for him. Watching him eat was, well, it was quite trying. I was so uncomfortable seeing him grasp a coffee cup with both hands and watching the slow, shaky journey the cup took to his mouth.

I will eliminate the long pauses between the words of our conversation for two reasons. One, to keep writing in the halting way Kyle spoke would increase the pages of this book so much that I'd have to raise the price of the book. And two, what he said next hit me with such force that I don't want you to be distracted by my creative antics in sentence patterns.

Kyle said, "I have your hiking book on the headboard of my bed. Every night I touch it and say, 'I will write a book someday.' Can you help me do it?"

With every fiber of my being I wanted to be elsewhere. *Dear God, how can I possibly help this young man when I can't even understand him unless I watch his mouth closely and guess at what he's saying?*

I thought it would just be too hard. But God didn't let me off the hook just because I was uncomfortable.

I gave Kyle some advice and reluctantly agreed to meet again the following week.

The morning of our next meeting, I was driving toward our meeting place.

Jesus, I don't want to do this for Kyle. It's too difficult.

What happened next removed all remaining goat tendencies from my life. I heard it so plainly in my spirit: *Paul, you're not doing it for Kyle. You're doing it for Me. Kyle is someone's son; he could be your son. Wouldn't you want someone to help your son? Kyle is My son.*

"Oh, dear Jesus, how selfish of me. Forgive my reluctant spirit!" I said aloud.

I wept tears of repentance for my selfish attitude.

I was drying tears as I entered the coffee shop. That morning, Kyle became my son, too.

"Kyle, I'll not only help you, but I'll ask my editor if she will assist you, too."

"But... I... have no... mon... ey."

"You don't need any. We won't charge you at all. Just give me a book when it's written."

My editor and I met with Kyle a few times, and he started writing. He wrote and he wrote and he wrote some more. He's been writing a column for a local newspaper now for several years. Writing for him is very tedious. He has other folks assist as well, especially his mom. He's also worked extremely hard on his enunciation. I've told him that when the book comes out, he will be giving talks, and he's vastly improved his speech.

I can understand him quite easily now, not because he has improved so much but because I want to understand him. I understand him because he's a sheep, and we sheep can communicate well. We communicate because we are following a Shepherd who communicates with us as well.

The Shepherd reminds us that what we do for others, we do for Him.

Kyle no longer goes to my church. But I see him often at either his place of employment or the local grocery store where we both frequent the café. He has a girlfriend, has just purchased a house, and is getting married this fall. When I spoke to him recently, he informed me his manuscript is finished and is scheduled to be published as his long-dreamed-of book.

Do you have a Kyle in your sphere of influence? There's someone you could help, I'm sure of it—but it might take an effort. You might have to sacrifice some comfort. These folks are sons and daughters of our Almighty God. That makes them your sons and daughters as well.

Can you even imagine the joy Kyle will experience when he holds that first book in his hands? He can take my book down from his headboard. He will replace it with his own and say, "I did it!" I'm so proud of Kyle. I love Kyle as a son. If Kyle can follow his dream, what's holding you back?

> Then the King will say to those on His right, "Come, blessed of my Father, take your inheritance, the

Kingdom prepared for you since the creation of the world. For I desired to write a book and you helped me. I was too poor to afford a good education, and you offered me scholarships. I was a single girl and pregnant, and you took me in. You saved my child. I was paralyzed, in a prison of my room, and you purchased a comfortable bed. When I needed transportation, you donated a van for me."

Then the sheep will say, "Lord, when did we see you wanting to write a book? When did we see you pregnant and scared? When did we see you without an education? When did we see you paralyzed, or needing a vehicle?"

The King will reply, "I tell you the truth, whatever you did for one of the least of these, you did for me."

    The least of these folks are all around you. You can do the least or you can do the most for these people. For some of these least folks, it's you and only you who can help.
    Don't wait too long to be Jesus to someone.

71

Who Is Your Neighbor?

Jesus was being questioned by an expert. What's an expert? Someone who knows less than those of us who know more. The expert in Luke 10 met the man who knew more that day. He was an expert in law, a lawyer. Of course, he knew more!

(Insert your favorite lawyer jokes here. I'll refrain. It's a Sunday morning as I write this, and I'm filled with kindness. Neighborly kindness.)

This lawyer wanted to test Jesus. He wanted to show Jesus his skills, his expertise in all things legal. Based on the language of his questions, he may have been an inheritance lawyer.

"Teacher," he asked, "what are the requirements to inherit eternal life?"

"You tell me," Jesus countered. "You're the expert in law. How do you understand it?"

Brimming with confidence, the lawyer recited the "right" answer: "Love the Lord your God with all your heart and with all your soul and with all your strength and with all your mind; and love your neighbor as yourself."

"You are correct," Jesus said. "Follow this dictate, and you will live."

Had the lawyer just nodded and pretended to understand, he could have walked away feeling good about himself. But he did what so many experts do. He kept talking after he had exhausted his expertise.

"Oh, teacher, who is my neighbor?"

Jesus was two steps ahead of this lawyer and had the answer ready.

Sure, Jesus could easily have told him quickly who his neighbor was, but Jesus, being a storyteller, gave the lawyer the truth in story form.

A man needed to get from Jerusalem to Jericho. He left Jerusalem, passing over the Mount of Olives. From this vantage point, he would have had one final grand view of the city of Jerusalem. Continuing on his eighteen-mile journey, he would pass Bethany. Then the road headed sharply downhill.

Jerusalem stands at 2,500 feet above sea level. It really is a city on a hill. Jericho is 825 feet below sea level. The steepness of the dramatic elevation loss turned this into a treacherous journey. The man was in a hurry, for reasons unknown. He could have taken other longer and safer routes, but he did not.

Thirteen miles toward Jericho, he reached the danger zone. Five miles out was a pass called Ascent of Blood. Some say it's so called because of the red rocks in the area. The more believable reason for the name is that much blood was shed by the robbers who often hid in the rocks and lay in wait for victims. I can imagine a traveler approaching that area with fear and trepidation. If he could only get through this pass, he could see the outskirts of Jericho and Herod's winter castle towering over the city.

The traveler of Jesus' story did not get through the pass safely. He was attacked, beaten up, and robbed. The robbers left him half dead. Fortunately, that also left him half alive.

A preacher man soon came down the road. He gave the suffering man a wide berth. I'm guessing he had a revival meeting planned for Jericho and needed to meet with the planning committee.

Then a Levite came along. When the children of Israel reached the Promised Land, the tribe of Levi was not given any land. They were in charge of serving God in the tabernacle and later in the temple. Their responsibilities included transporting the tabernacle and all the holy objects whenever the children of Israel moved to a new location. In the temple, they were the ones who opened and closed all the gates. In other words, they were important, set apart. The Levite would have been too enamored with the logistics of church planning and planting to be troubled with one person. One can certainly see why he would pass by a naked, injured man. That "situation" in the ditch alongside the road was really the responsibility of another committee.

A Samaritan came along, and he did stop. Samaritans and Jews hated each other. Why would this man stop? He took pity on the man in such dire need. That's so encouraging to me. Kindness overcame hatred that day.

The Samaritan bandaged up the injured man, loaded him on his donkey, and took him to an inn. He even remained with the wounded man overnight, and the following day gave the innkeeper cash, with a promise to return to see if any additional expenses had been incurred for the man's care.

We could stop there and have learned a lesson, but Jesus hadn't made His point yet. He turned to the lawyer and asked the question He's asking you as well: "Which of these three was actually being a neighbor to the man who was in need?"

"The one who showed mercy to him," replied the expert.

"Now you know, go do it."

We tend to think of "our neighbors" as the family next door to us. Or those in the community in which we live. Or those who share a commonality with us.

But we need to expand our neighbor range a bit. Wherever we are in this wide world, we will have a neighbor. In the grocery store or in a hospital waiting room or at the airport. Wherever we travel, we will be on a Jericho road.

Can you love that person up ahead in need, or will you move to the other side and look the other way?

Can you love the unlovable? That person who disrupts your day? Those in your community who are viewed with contempt?

D.L. Moody once shared a story about a little boy who walked several miles to go to Sunday school. He passed by thirty other churches to get to one particular church. When he was asked why he passed by those other churches, he said, "This church knows how to love a little boy."

In Jesus' story, which of the three are you—the preacher man, the Levite, or the good Samaritan?

I would have to confess, I've been all three.

I've even been the man in the ditch, beaten and burdened. My burdens were sins. A Man came by and paid the price to redeem and heal me.

Here's a short parable of my own making.

A man is in Walmart. You see him from afar and recognize him as someone down on his luck. You could help him. Do you? Or do you dart down a side aisle instead? He's your neighbor.

Or you walk into church and recognize a visitor—someone you've wronged in the past. The Holy Spirit prompts you that a loving apology is required. Do you find a seat on the opposite side of the sanctuary? He's your neighbor.

Haven't we all darted down a side aisle or looked away and walked in the other direction? I only need to look in a mirror to see a man guilty of that.

Who is *your* neighbor?

Be that good Samaritan, because someday you will need a good Samaritan.

Don't wait too long.

72

Weary Pilgrim

The first five days of my Appalachian Trail hike were brutal. I had left the comforts of a soft bed and warm showers for sleeping on the hard forest floor and showers that were raindrops from above—or snow and sleet.

Five days was enough. I needed a break. I needed a good Samaritan to rescue me and take me to an inn and give me a cup of cold water. I needed my soul restored.

I had already walked by still waters—and had waters dumped on me in the form of rain, snow, and sleet. I had lain down in green forests, exhausted. I felt as though I had walked through the valley of the shadow of death. But the Blueberry Patch hostel did indeed restore my soul.

The hostel near Hiawassee, Georgia, is no longer in existence, but back in 2008, Gary and Lennie Poteet saved my hike. Because they were disciples of Jesus, they gave me that cup of cold water. They took me into their inn, fed me, gave me a warm bed, and even laundered my clothes. Running the hostel as a ministry, they served Jesus by serving everyone who came to their door, weary and hungry.

I surely do owe them. I was ready to quit. If I would have given up then, I never would have launched into the new life that the Appalachian Trail and *Hiking Through* opened for me. I pray that goodness and love will follow them all the days of their lives.

It was Easter Sunday morning. At the Blueberry Patch, a breakfast table was prepared for the twelve hikers gathered there. Gary led in a prayer and a devotional. We ate and we ate. Then we ate some more. A hiker burns 7,000 calories daily while hiking the Appalachian Trail. A person going about a normal day (which we surely were not) burns about 2,000 calories a day. As hikers, we could rarely eat enough to sustain our hungry bodies. When given the chance, we ate all we could hold. That morning, we had a chance, and we took it.

Gary noted my trail name and invited me to go to church with them. What Baptist church wouldn't want an Apostle to show up on Easter Sunday?

I declined the invitation. I was hiking with buddies and didn't want to lose them by staying off the trail that morning, but I promised I'd return some day and go to church with Gary and Lennie. I had no idea when or under what circumstances I would return, but I knew I would someday.

God moves in mysterious ways. It would be years before I returned. I had two thousand more miles to hike on that trail and lots of other living to do before I would keep my promise. All I was aware of that weekend was that the Blueberry Patch had provided exactly what I needed at the time. However, God had a plan that reached even further than my immediate needs, and he had already set the plan in motion.

73

The Eternal Gift

Sometimes in life, what seems like a chance encounter is God at work, setting up a chain of events yet to follow, like a line of dominoes being set up, ready for one event to push itself into the next and the next and the next.

So it was on that day in Sikeston, Missouri. As at the Blueberry Patch, I had no idea what God was up to. I was only aware of what I saw immediately in front of me. Now, looking back over the years, I see God's hand in each event.

I was on my bicycle, heading to Key West, Florida. I had already pedaled three thousand miles from my starting point in the northwest corner of Washington State. That morning in Sikeston, Missouri, I needed to make a choice of routes. My destination that day was Paducah, Kentucky, but I had optional routes to getting there. I was considering State Route 62, because Ohio's State Route 62 passes directly through my home town. Home was calling me that morning. I was tempted to turn my bicycle in that direction and not stop until I was home. I was getting quite lonely, pedaling alone mile after mile.

At the front desk of the motel, I inquired about the best route towards Paducah. The receptionist said the interstate would be the most direct route. Riding a bicycle on interstates is frowned upon. However, if I could ride 17 miles on the interstate without getting arrested, I would reach a small country road taking me directly into Paducah.

It was Sunday morning, and traffic would be not be too heavy. I did approach the on ramp with a bit of apprehension. A bit of fear mixed with an adrenalin rush as I wondered if I could avoid Missouri's finest.

A hitchhiker stood at the ramp to the interstate. He held a sign indicating he was headed to New Orleans. A bit unkempt, he looked like the kind of guy you'd probably cross the Jericho Road to avoid.

I stopped my bike and wished the man a good morning.

"Why did you stop to talk to me?" he wondered. "Most folks are afraid of me."

"Why would I be afraid of you? The only bad thing you could do is steal my bike. Then you would have transportation and I could go home." Pointing to the seat, I exclaimed, "That seat is a torture rack."

We chatted a while, and then he asked me a question.

"How is it possible to be pedaling across America by yourself and yet have a look of peace on your face?"

"I have that peace because I'm not alone. I have a relationship with Jesus, and He is always with me. That's why I can do this ride alone."

"I don't have that peace," he reflected with a sorrowful look. "If only I did." He went on to tell me he had just been released from prison for selling drugs. He admitted he was guilty. While he was in prison, his wife divorced him and his son committed suicide. "I am a failure," he said.

He was hitchhiking to the Gulf Coast to find a job, sleeping under bridges at night. He showed me a book of poems he had composed during those lonely times. He was a talented man, but hopelessly lost.

"God can forgive all your failures," I told him. "There is redemption available for you."

As I was leaving, I reached into my pocket and handed him a $20 bill.

"I didn't ask for your money," he said.

"I know you didn't ask. And you don't have to earn it. It's a free gift."

As I pedaled away, tears were running down his face.

Did he recognize the meaning of a free gift?

Do you recognize and understand the meaning of free gift? The result of that free gift is a face that shows peace and contentment. Peace, even when alone and lonely.

Peace in the heart shows on the face. Can people see that the Holy Spirit dwells within you?

God's free gift will take you to eternity and last forever. This beautiful gift has a lifetime warranty plus an extended warranty for all eternity. Accept it, while it's being freely given.

Don't wait too long.

Godly Investments

The best investment a person can make is investing in other people's lives. We can do that in various ways. Acts of kindness. Being at a sick person's bedside. During the latter stages of my wife's life, she had several friends who gave of their time so freely; they were the hands and feet of Jesus to both Mary and me. Helping someone in need, either physically or financially. Even simply being available to talk to a lonely person is an investment for eternity.

I had invested $20 in a homeless man who couldn't repay me. It felt good to know I made a $20 difference in a man's life. Maybe those seeds I planted about the free gift would take root.

I gave no thought to being rewarded for my generosity. My reward was the peace I felt in giving a gift that couldn't be repaid. However, when you do business with the bank of God, the terms aren't always easily defined. God can repay or bless as He pleases. And what He does with our investments will be beyond anything we expect.

Weeks before, on the second day of my cross-country bike ride, I had found a dime on the shoulder of Highway 101 in the state of Washington. I stopped to pick it up and decided to pick up all the money I found on America's highways. From the corner of Washington to Key West Florida, I did just that.

The shoulders of America's highway are a veritable hardware store. Besides money, I could find anything and everything at this roadside shopping mall. I picked up a variety of items, attempting to cushion my bike seat. A found screwdriver came in handily when the bike chain jammed at the Golden Gate Bridge.

My favorite roadside finds were always money.

Pedaling through a little town in Kentucky, I spied a money clip resting on the shoulder. It was silver and held what appeared to be several dollars. I stuffed it into my pocket without actually removing the cash.

That evening, I was already in bed in Paris when I remembered I had found money but never checked to see how much the money clip actually held.

Wait, did you say Paris?

Yes, Paris, Tennessee. (It just sounded more sophisticated to say "Paris.")

I climbed out of bed to retrieve my roadside gift. To my surprise, the clip did hold several dollar bills. Inside the singles were several twenties, and inside the twenties were seven one-hundred-dollar bills. I had just found the currency equivalent of Russian nesting dolls.

Yes, you read that correctly.

As I stuffed the money back inside its silver domicile, I was reminded of the $20 I'd given the homeless hitchhiker. He could never repay me, but God could. God's bank has generous terms. I had found 37 times as much money as I had given away.

Since I believe God has a sense of humor, I thanked Him for the money and remarked that I probably should have given the homeless man $40!

75

Return to Blueberry Patch

The silver money clip containing the highway bounty was brought home and stashed away in a drawer. I did call the police to report what I had found. They said no one had reported it missing, so it was mine to keep.

My desire, though, was to give it away. It was a free gift to me, and I was so blessed that day when I found it that I wanted to bless somebody else with it.

For three years, it lay in my drawer. My spirit received no prompting about a worthy cause or person to receive it.

Then the year arrived when I planned to kayak the Mississippi River. As you may recall, that choice is still on my Top-Five Stupid Choices in Life list. The kayak I chose (that would eventually save my life) was expensive. I remembered the money lying in my drawer. I would use that as a partial payment on the kayak, I thought.

That seemed to get the Holy Spirit's attention.

That's not what that money is for.

"Pray, tell?"

The Blueberry Patch Hostel. Give it to them. Remember how they saved your hike on the Appalachian Trail? You were there on Easter Sunday. You promised to return someday and go to church with them. It's time to repay. Take it and give it to them.

Remember, this was six years after my stop at the Blueberry Patch. Six years!

But I could not ignore God's instructions. I called the Blueberry Patch and asked if I could visit and assist around the hostel.

"Sure, come on down," I was told.

In the details that only God can orchestrate, it was again Easter Sunday when I sat at Gary and Lennie's breakfast table the second time. I asked if I would be allowed to speak, and I presented them with the money and told the story of finding it in Paris, Tennessee. To my surprise, Gary had lived in Paris. He had hiked the Appalachian Trail and realized a need to be Jesus to hikers, so he moved to Hiawassee, Georgia, and bought the Blueberry Patch property.

As usual, Gary had a prayer before breakfast was served. His prayer that Easter Sunday morning was very personal, calling God "Our daddy." Unknown to any of us, a young lady hiker at the table was longing for just that—a daddy.

After breakfast, I offered rides to anyone who needed transportation back to the trail.

I also wanted to hike a few miles of the Appalachian Trail myself. Six years ago on an Easter Sunday I had hiked through there, and I was in the grip of nostalgia.

As I labored up a steep hill, I heard sounds of weeping behind me. It was Jill, the young lady hiker I had met at the breakfast table earlier that morning. I paused, waiting for her to catch up with me. She was weeping inconsolably.

During my years in management, I've listened to employees' stories of hardship and sadness. I've empathized with hurting people in tears. My story of losing my spouse has given me opportunity to weep with many others who weep. I especially know the difficulty of hiking that trail, alone in the woods with only the company of sad thoughts and broken dreams. I'd shed my share of tears on the Appalachian Trail, too.

"Jill, I don't know why you're crying, but just know that when I hiked this trail, I often cried, too. Especially at night in my tent. It can get really lonely out here."

"That's not why I'm crying," she said. "That's not why I'm so sad."

"I don't know if I can help you or not, but I'll gladly listen."

"This morning, when I listened to the prayer at that breakfast table, this horrible pain hit me. Gary prayed, 'God, you are our daddy.' I want that so badly. I want a daddy that loves me. I hate my dad. He left Mom and us children when we were young. I hate him! I hate my entire family."

"I'm sorry your dad did that to you. But God really does want to be your daddy. He'll never leave you or reject you."

Jill had just returned from serving in Afghanistan. She didn't want to return to her home state of Wisconsin, where her mother lived. She and her mom didn't get along; her father had destroyed that relationship, too. She ended up staying in Maine with friends.

One of those friends gave her a book about a man who hiked the Appalachian Trail and found peace. Jill read about half the book and decided to hike the trail herself, in search of that elusive peace.

"That's why I'm out here in the middle of the woods, crying about having no daddy," she said.

"What was the title of that book you were reading?" I asked. But I suspected I already knew.

"*Hiking Through.*"

"Jill, do you realize how much God, your daddy, loves you? You're standing in the middle of the woods, talking to the person who wrote that book."

Jill looked at me with astonishment. "You are kidding me."

"Not kidding. I wrote it after hiking this trail and finding peace after my wife died of cancer."

When we parted ways, I told Jill I would pray she found the same peace I had found on the Appalachian Trail. I told her once again that God, her loving daddy, would never leave her. We exchanged contact information and she promised to keep me informed about her progress toward peace.

I returned to the Blueberry Patch and excitedly told Gary about my conversation with Jill and how his prayer using "our daddy" had affected her.

"Apostle," he said, addressing me with my original trail name, "I pray around that breakfast table every morning. This was the first time I ever used that term. This morning in prayer, the Holy Spirit told me to use 'our daddy' today."

Friends, do you still question the power of hearing from God through the Holy Spirit within us? God speaks to our Holy Spirit in spiritual thoughts that the Spirit interprets for us.

How often do you hear that still voice whisper a suggestion to call someone? How often do you have a name instilled in your consciousness and wonder why? Have you heard anything from the Holy Spirit lately?

Would God really send me to the Blueberry Patch in the very first week of my Appalachian Trail hike? Would God really have me meet a homeless man on the interstate in

Missouri years later? Would God really prompt me to give him $20? Would He really have me find a large amount of money on a highway in Kentucky? Would He really have me go back to the Blueberry Patch to gift them that money? Would God really ask Gary to change his prayer language for one morning? Would God orchestrate all that just to have me meet one lost, lonely soul seeking a daddy?

These aren't chance encounters. God loves us all so much He will set up a series of events intended to reach a troubled soul. As we walk the narrow way with our Guide, Jesus asks us to take our part in the plans. We may think our action insignificant. We may think it affects no one but ourselves. We may think a simple act or a prayer has no results. But did you know that Paul wrote in 1 Corinthians 15:58 that *nothing* we do for the Lord is ever useless? If your Guide prompts you, He has a purpose.

Are you willing to be included in His plans? Is there a lonely Jill somewhere in your sphere of influence? Will you meet her on her trail of despair at just the appointed moment? I was willing. I'm so glad I didn't wait too long.

The Redemption of Jill

Jill reached out to me a few times over the following weeks. She carried a heavy burden of loneliness and sadness. She wanted to quit her hike but had nowhere to call home. I encouraged her to go back home and try to make peace with her mom. She doubted that was possible but agreed to try. Her attempt to reconnect met with limited success. The damage her dad had done to the entire family had severe and lasting consequences.

She left home and couch-surfed at numerous friends' homes. Occasionally she would call me from a bar and I'd learn of the bad choices she was making. "Jill, you need to find a church and get your life in order," I told her repeatedly.

One Sunday morning I was in my church pew, listening to the Sunday morning message. I had the good sense to have my phone silenced, yet I felt the vibration of a text coming in. I discreetly read the text. Was that okay to do in church?

We have several doctors in church, and I imagine they need to read their texts in case of emergency. I'm sort of like a doctor. Sort of. I'm a soul doctor, and Jill was my patient.

The text was from Jill. She was in a type of hospital. She was in church—a hospital for sinners needing a transfusion. She needed a soul cleansing. She needed the blood of Jesus that cleanses from all unrighteousness.

However, the blood type she needed was not available that day. The text read: "I'm sitting in church frustrated and disgusted. The pastor is preaching about marriage and families. None of that interests me. Why am I even here? There's no reason to go to church."

Discretion was no longer important. My patient needed help STAT! (That's a medical term used often in a hospital. It's Latin for *statim* meaning *immediately*.)

My patient needed help NOW! I quickly texted back a prescription: "Get yourself to another church. Find a church that preaches forgiveness of sins. A church where you can find redemption."

A few more months went by. One Sunday evening, another text came from Jill. This one brought tears to my eyes.

"Paul, I got saved. I was baptized tonight! I've been redeemed!"

Redeemed. One of my favorite words. Purchased back from a life of sin by a sacrifice made on a cross.

Jill had discovered and been given the correct blood type.

How much did God love Jill? Two people with diverse backgrounds, traveling different pathways—yet those pathways intersected in the Georgia woods. I was raised in a godly home with a godly dad. Jill couldn't wait to leave home because she hated her dad. Her pathway led her from Wisconsin to Afghanistan to Maine to the Georgia woods. Mine went from Ohio to a thru-hike on the Appalachian Trail to a bike ride across America to finding money in Kentucky to another walk in the Georgia woods.

There is no Rolex watch in the world with better precision timing than God's timing. Only He can orchestrate such a series of events. Only He could make money scooped up from a highway in Kentucky lead to a baptism in North Dakota.

There were 99 sheep safely back in the fold. One was missing. Jill was lost in the woods. Jesus left the 99 safely in the fold and went after her. He redeemed her and welcomed her home.

Home to Daddy!

77

Mystery in the Mist

Here is a truth about our walk with God: the enemy will try to derail us in any way he can. Peter wrote that we need to stay alert and on guard; the devil prowls around like a roaring lion, looking for those he can devour (see 1 Peter 5:8). He's not content with just snapping at our heels or being an annoying pest. He has destruction on his agenda. He intends to gobble us up.

I suspected it was Satan's doing, sending old thoughts back into my head for long into the night. What little sleep came stayed briefly and then fled once again. My mind was a figure-8 racetrack with thoughts circling fast and endlessly. The little mind cars zoomed around my brain, with every circuit flashing the labels of their sponsors before my weary eyes and brain.

Here comes deception around the backtrack.

Rejection has the inside lane, and oh—what a daring move! Rejection passes deception and gains on broken trust.

Now all three are side by side. Broken trust is forced into the wall and what a disaster! That car is demolished. Those sponsors will never trust that driver again.

Deception wins by a nose. A nose growing ever larger with the passing of time.

Rejection finishes second. That's often the case with rejection.

Then came my Counselor's voice: *Get up, oh modern-day Enoch. You need a God walk.*

So this writer found himself alone on the local walking trail very early in the morning.

"God, speak to me."

Off in the distance, I saw what appeared to be a brilliant white doorway. It was indeed an entrance, the entrance to a fogbank. It reminded me of a door into the unknown.

As I approached this white-mist doorway, the pathway became a bit clearer, but still foggy.

At a road crossing, I stopped at the stop sign posted there. I can sense when the Holy Spirit wants my attention. Perhaps it's also my desire for the Holy Spirit to put me in touch with God.

I waited.

I listened.

I felt God saying, *Do you trust Me? It's easy to trust when life is sunny and all is well.*

How about when trust is broken and the pathway ahead is unclear?

Do you trust Me to walk with you through those foggy times in life?

Do you trust Me enough to walk through that door of uncertainty into the unknown?

"God, I'm trying really hard to trust You. I say I do, but honestly, some days it seems as if I'm alone, lost in the fog.

"But I will trust in You because You promised to never leave or forsake me."

Tears came for a while, then I felt comforted as God and I walked into the mist together.

And since I didn't get translated like Enoch, I returned home and wrote about the mysteries of walking with God.

78

Heroes

"Heroes are in short supply today." You've probably heard or read that dire analysis as many times as I have. Perhaps you agree. It used to be that your dad was your hero. Some dads still are heroes to their children. Mine most definitely was. But many dads have abdicated that role. Those in the media spotlights who are called "heroes" are often standing on cracked and shaky pedestals.

My image of *hero*, sad to say, had lost its power. Then God adjusted my spectacles a bit and I'm seeing things differently right now.

Several weeks ago, I met a hero. He tells me he met one, too—when he met me.

I'll tell you, it was odd hearing him say that. I've never felt like a hero. A hero rushes into a burning building to save a life. A hero is the neurosurgeon who removed half of my nine-year-old grandson's skull to save his life.

Is a person who writes words for a living a hero if these words change lives? Is he a hero if those words bring a man to Jesus? If so, then I humbly and gratefully accept the title.

This meeting of heroes occurred because a man from Boston read my book *Hiking Through,* and it changed his life. The book inspired him to hike the Appalachian Trail, but then he came up with another idea. He determined to walk across America to raise money and awareness for veteran causes.

When he walked through my hometown and discovered the writer of *Hiking Through* lived there, he wanted to meet me. I was his hero.

I picked him up as he walked alongside the highway and took him to breakfast. We tried to determine who was the bigger hero to the other, but we soon realized there were more heroes close by.

A group of retirees sat at a corner table. Several of the men wore hats with service insignias. My walker hero approached their table, and soon stories were told in rapid succession.

These heroes are fortunate. They can talk about their times overseas. Many heroes' voices were silenced as they served their country.

So many heroes in one small country café. Had it not been breakfast, we would have ordered hero sandwiches.

My hiker buddy was a teacher before he retired. He told us about a writing assignment he gave his students one day: Write a two-page paper that makes you cry.

Wow! What an assignment. At first thought, you might think it's nearly impossible. But I understood what he meant. In my writing life, I have done it often. It happens most frequently when I feel the Holy Spirit directing me on what to write.

Think about your life. Have you ever spoken words that made another cry? Have you ever cried at the memory of a song? Have you ever wept when you opened a card and read just a few handwritten, heartfelt words? That's the beautiful power of well-arranged or well-spoken words.

Try it sometime. Write something that makes you cry. Perhaps write about your hero. Write about your dad or mom. Write about a friend who has passed out of this life. You might even write about your favorite pet that is no longer with you.

As I mentioned previously, I have written words that made me cry. However, a first occurred when I was moved to write "The Alabaster Heart." That morning, I cried before I even started writing.

I had read the account in the book of Luke the previous day, but I had no desire or plan to write about it. When I knelt to pray the next morning, I felt compelled to write about the story of the woman living in sin. I couldn't even continue praying. *Do it now.* The tears came before I was even off my knees.

That is the story of a lady who needed a hero. She found one that day.

Some heroes serve their countries, some write words, some walk across America. Some preach, some teach, some are busy mothers. I'm suddenly seeing far more heroes than I ever imagined.

Are you a hero to someone? It really doesn't take that much effort.

Don't wait too long.

Lights in the Valley

When I decided to hike the Appalachian Trail, I needed a trail name. All thru-hikers either choose a name or are given one. Your legally given name is left behind as you start out in the wilderness, and on the trail you will be known by your trail name only. Oftentimes, I didn't even know my fellow hikers' real first names.

I chose the trail name Apostle. I knew this name risked me being immediately categorized as some type of holy man. I chose the name because of the meaning of *apostle:* "one sent forth with a message."

After Mary passed away, I realized how much she had done for our family. I had taken it for granted. I assumed that when I returned from work, the floors would be cleaned, the dishes washed, and the laundry done. Since I was at work much of the time, I seldom saw all this happen. I can't say what I thought—did I believe leprechauns or the shoemaker's elves did all the work? Truth be told, I never thought much about it. But if it was leprechauns or elves, they left with Mary. And then, I was doing it all myself. I am sorry to say that raising our children was much the same—I took for granted that they were in good care and would be properly taught by my wife. I missed so much of both the laughter and tears of my children's early years.

When we're in the middle of living, we often forget to really live, to enjoy the now. Too often, we think we will enjoy life *someday*, some distant time when the house is paid for, the kids are grown, and life is perfectly in order.

If you are running through life right now with that perspective, allow me to predict your future. Someday you will stop and look back, and you'll realize the best living was when the children were growing up. You were coming and going from work, school, church, ballgames, and all the activities that filled your calendar, and the best of life was going on without you.

That was the message I intended to carry with me on the Appalachian hike. I determined to use the trail name "Apostle" and deliver this reminder to men not to take their spouses or families for granted. I thought my great loss had taught me much, but the trail taught me even more...

Another hiker and I were camped atop Humpback Mountain in Virginia's Shenandoah Park. Our tent sites were in a small grassy area not too far from a cliff that overlooked a vast valley.

I was already in my tent, cooking my meal for the evening, when I heard my friend calling me. "Hey, Apostle! You need to get out here and see this view."

I grabbed my food and joined him on the rocky ledge. Indentations in the rock formation offered great seats that still held warmth from the sun. I settled into my seat as the evening coolness wrapped around us.

Beneath us lay the Shenandoah Valley. It was a breathtaking sight. Far off on the horizon, the sun was swiftly sinking down behind a mountain range. Across the valley, lights started to flicker in homes. Street lights came on. Car headlights curved through neighborhoods, finding their way home. I envisioned children already home from school and moms preparing meals. Families were coming together after another busy day.

The sun set. Life moved indoors. Some families laughed. Some families loved. Some families were mourning loss. Birthdays were celebrated. Anniversaries toasted. Without doubt, some arguments were heating up. I hoped forgiveness was also being offered. I wondered if those families realized they were in the middle of life, of living. Or were they missing the blessings of now? If we fail to live in the moment, we'll miss experiencing the true meaning of life.

Life teemed below us as the sun set and darkness veiled the features of the valley. The world was shadowy and dim—except for those lights of life.

Then, in the air between us and the life below, fireflies began their night of living. Millions of little yellow lights blinked on and off, on and off. I imagined they blinked praise to their Creator and a message of hope for humanity. They blinked a message of encouragement to two sojourners on a pilgrimage, watching from above. Yes, they let their little lights shine. Lights in the darkness.

Could we Christians be a bit more like those fireflies?

> Let your light shine before men, that they may see your good deeds and praise your Father in heaven.
> Matthew 5:16 (AP)

80

And Then What?

Have you ever been engrossed in a book, reading along, and suddenly a misdirection is tossed in? I'll do that occasionally in my writing. Even the Bible has instances of those interruptions.

Second Kings 13 is a prime example. In that chapter, Elisha and the king of Israel are having an archery exhibition of sorts. It was not a competition in which they competed against each other. Elisha was on his deathbed when the king came to visit him. The prophet made several odd requests, but the king never questioned them. He obeyed. Elisha then used the exercise to deliver prophecy about the king's battles with Israel's enemies. It's a strange and intriguing story. Look it up.

Then, suddenly, we read about a burial. Verses 20 and 21 dip into an even more intriguing story that has no satisfying ending. A man had died. He was dead. A genuine, bona fide goner. These two verses start as the burial is taking place.

It's springtime, the time for new life to appear. What a spring this man had! Newness of life, just as spring should be. But I'm getting ahead of the story (all two verses of it).

We learn two things in the first two lines: Elisha had died. And springtime also brought raiders from neighboring Moab to the land of Israel, ransacking the countryside.

The dead man was being buried when those responsible for the body saw a band of raiders approaching. They panicked and tossed the body into a tomb nearby and, I would imagine, ran for home. This was Elisha's tomb, and the body landed atop Elisha's bones. Immediately, the dead man was jolted back to life and stood to his feet.

Talk about powerful dead bones!

And that's the end of the account in 2 Kings 13. No! I want more. What happened to him when he returned to town? Don't you want to know? I do.

One of the books on my to-do list will be titled *And Then What?* If that manuscript ever comes to fruition, it will be these fascinating stories from the Bible. There are many such accounts that tease my curiosity. I want to know what happened next, but we are not told.

Can you imagine the shock in town when the body they carried out to the burial grounds comes waltzing down the street? The folks at the town gate sipping their goat's milk and nibbling on cheese will be dumbfounded. Word spreads quickly. This man left dead but comes back alive.

And then what? Well, I visualize the doctors' offices will close. There will be no need for their expertise in that town anymore. If someone dies, take him out to the tomb and toss him on Elisha's bones. It will be known as the town where no one stays dead. Other towns will want to avail themselves of those bones as well. I mean, how would you keep such a thing secret? Or, perhaps, there was only enough power for one resurrection. Even so, what would that man's life be like until his next death?

My imagination goes on and on with possible scenarios. I do, however, have a point to make.

J. Vernon McGee (1904-1988) was a theologian and a radio minister. He wrote a series of Bible commentaries covering every book in the Bible, and he occasionally used anecdotes to make a point. When writing about Samson and his great strength, McGee described how Samson had picked up a jawbone from a dead donkey and used that as a weapon to kill 1,000 Philistines. If Samson and God could do that with a dead donkey, wrote McGee, imagine what He could do with alive donkeys like you and me!

That's a bit insulting, to be sure, but I take no offense.

And here's the point of all this: If you are alive (and since you're reading this, I presume you are), if you're a Christian (which I don't assume you are), do you have enough power in your live bones to resurrect a sinner tossed your way?

You should have. It's the mission we've been given as followers of Jesus.

I see this book in your hands as a skeleton of sorts. A bone pile, if you wish. If you're dead and being held captive in sin, this pile of bones you've been tossed into can bring springtime to your life. A new life. A changed life. A godly life.

It's not my words that have the power to resurrect you. My words are just a signpost, pointing the way. The way is Jesus. Allow Him to bring the Holy Spirit into your own life and find new life for your bones.

With the Holy Spirit inside, your "and then what" story will be amazing and powerful!

81

God of Truth

I thrive on truth. I was raised on it. You did not lie in our household. The punishment for an exposed lie was worse than the lie itself. Lying just wasn't worth it.

Lest I sound perfect, I will admit to one lie I told my dad. I lied to avoid an extreme punishment, and for a brief moment, I thought lying wasn't so bad, after all. The thought only lasted for one minute, though, because it only took one minute for the lie to be exposed.

That day, my friend had come home with me after morning church services. He was going to spend the afternoon with me. We often did that, back in the day when most churches had a service in the morning and one in the evening.

My buddy and I scurried up the road, seeking cigarette butts with enough remaining tobacco to light. Yes, I know. It does sound so disgusting.

Sequestered in my bedroom with the door closed and the window open, we lit those little discarded devil sticks.

A knock sounded on the door.

"Are you guys smoking in there?" My father didn't sound very happy.

"No, Dad." *Of course not.*

Flick, flick. Quickly our little roaches were sent sailing through the open window. And I had just successfully pulled a fast one on Dad.

Actually, I had not. That brief minute I mentioned was up.

"Open up now!" exclaimed my father. What happened to knocking and politely requesting admission?

I opened. There stood Dad with the two little smoldering stubs we had so diligently sought out.

"He did it." "He did it." Our quick blame shifting didn't work.

I'm sure my dad reported to my friend's dad later that evening after church. I don't recall what my friend's punishment was, but I'd prefer not to talk about mine.

Suffice it to say, I never lied to Dad again.

When people tell us something, whether it's in the workplace, or at home, or in a relationship, we base our response on the assumption of truth. We learn quickly who we can trust to tell us the truth. And who we will not trust. Wouldn't it be nice if everyone just spoke truth? It would make life so much easier.

There is one who always speaks truth. Jesus said He was truth. 1 John 5:20 says, "And we know also that the Son of God has come and has given us understanding, so that we may know him who is true."

It's amazing to me how often Jesus' inner circle didn't understand what He meant. Many were fishermen, so I suppose they weren't intellectuals like you or I. I'm joking, you're not an intellectual! And I'll admit it, I'm not either. I'm a lot like those fishermen. Just an average, normal man. But that's who Jesus used and uses.

I'm often amazed that Jesus can use me. He does because He knows if something needs to be written, I'll write it. My writing will never be praised among the intellectual community. My books will never be listed among the bestsellers written by pompous paragons of parody. (Okay, so I'm not even sure what that phrase means, but didn't it sound good?)

My simple writings, however, can lead to a changed life. My writings can show a person that Jesus is the way to eternal life. That's writing truth.

God will never lie to us (Titus 1:2). It's just not in His character. What's more, He wants us to know the truth. He'll tell us the truth as we walk and talk with Him.

Accept this gift from Him. Then give the gift of truth to everyone in your life, with truthful words and truthful living. A lie destroys. Truth heals.

Accept the greatest of truths and be truly healed.

Don't wait too long.

82

The Real Life

During my hike from Georgia to Maine, I met many people who had suffered great losses and pain. The Trail seems to send out a special call to those who need time to heal or sort things out. Some of the folks I met were in and out of my hike within a few miles; others stayed connected, and some became hiking partners on my journey and friends for life.

One man and I spoke one day about the loss of our spouses. For both of us, the loss was recent. After my friend's wife died, he realized that he had not seen the importance of daily life during the years he and his wife had together. He had not taken the joy available in daily interaction and love of family and friends. The couple had worked hard and become wealthy. But when faced with the end of his wife's life, in his hour of need, his possessions did not bring him satisfaction.

He got a glimpse of the life that is truly life and gave away most of his possessions, purchased a backpack, and went hiking. "If you can't carry it on your back or in your heart, you don't need it," he said.

Many people spend a great deal of time preparing to stay here on Earth. They spend their lifetime accumulating money and possessions for some future goal. But contentment is elusive. "Making a living" keeps them so busy, they don't really live. The Plan is to spend their waning years on earth enjoying the fruits of a lifetime of labor. They have traded the joy of the journey for a destination that is never guaranteed, and so often, sadly, that destination is never reached.

My friends, let's not miss out on leading a life that leads to the life that is truly life.

1 Timothy 6:6 speaks about godliness with contentment being "great gain." Do you have the courage to stand in front of a mirror and ask that person looking back at you for an honest answer to the question: "What do you consider great gain?"

I was born into, grew up in, and still live in an area of great affluence. Our community has a great work ethic, and that ethic combined with energetic entrepreneurship has created much wealth. Our community includes extremely wealthy folks, folks on their way to becoming rich, and those who want to get rich.

Do you have a great deal of this world's capital? Or does it seem as if everyone around you has wealth and you alone are struggling financially?

No matter where you see yourself on the poor-to-rich scale, God has a message for you in 1 Timothy 6. Folks who want to get rich are prime targets for temptations and traps that can take one to ruin and destruction.

It almost makes you glad you're broke, doesn't it? No, I didn't think so. It doesn't! But heed this cautionary word in your desires for more wealth. This is where we find the well-known verse that the love of money is a root of all kinds of evil. It is that love, that craving, that gluttony, if you will, for more money that gives rise to evil. If the desire for more money overshadows the desire for more of God, then money has become the master of a life. If money is more important than living out Jesus' principles of the Kingdom of Heaven, then, as Jesus' said in Luke 6:24, "Woe to you who are rich!" or, as one translation puts it, "What sorrow awaits you..."

So, those who want to be rich must be cautious of the trap, but what's a poor rich man to do?

God has a command for those who have accumulated wealth. Don't be arrogant. Don't put your hope in wealth; put your hope in God. Do good; be rich in good deeds. Be generous and willing to share.

Actually, those words apply to all of us. The rich, the want-to-be-rich, the almost-rich, and anyone with any resources can take this command to heart. Put your hope in God, not in your wealth. Be rich in the good you do, and be willing to share. Why? Because by doing that, we will be laying up treasures for the coming age. Treasures in Heaven.

Timothy calls that coming age, "the life that is truly life."

> But store up for yourself treasures in heaven, where moth and rust do not destroy, and where thieves do not break in and steal. For where your treasure is, there your heart will be also. (Matthew 6:20-21)

The bank of Heaven is open, awaiting your treasures. Those deposits you send ahead will pay dividends throughout all eternity. You can bank on that!

Invest now in the future life that is *truly life*. Don't wait too long.

83

Joint Heirs with Jesus

Imagine being summoned to the reading of a will because you are listed as a beneficiary. The will is opened and read, and you have just been handed the keys to the universe! You have everything you have ever dreamed of—and so much more.

"How is this possible?" you ask.

It is possible because we are children. Not just average children, but children of God. I love how the Scripture often calls us followers of Jesus "children."

Romans 8 says we are God's children, and if we are His children, we are His heirs. But it gets so very interesting. Paul also writes that we are co-heirs with Jesus.

Is that even possible?

The very first verse in the book of Hebrews tells us that God has made His Son "heir of all things." Jesus' inheritance is the whole universe. As joint-heirs, what belongs to Jesus also belongs to us. The universe is our inheritance!

My mind can't quite comprehend that, even as I write this. But let's try, anyway.

Will we really have everything that God has given Jesus?

1 John 3 says this: "How great is the love the Father has lavished on us, that we should be called children of God!" Then, for emphasis, John wrote, "and that is what we are!"

You can tell that John, the apostle, was very excited about this concept. He goes on to say that as children of God, what we *will be* has not been made known yet, "but we know when He appears, we shall be like Him, for we shall see Him as He is."

We shall be like Him? Again, my mind is boggled!

What will happen when we pass on from this life is unimaginable. If the Father lavishes love on us now as children, try to imagine the lavishing that awaits us! We really can't. Folks try to imagine it. Many have written books about Heaven. Some of those books are encouraging, but most are not. No writer can describe what awaits the believer. The words we know cannot describe it, and our finite minds cannot conceive what awaits.

What I can and do comprehend is that God loves me and wants what is best for me in this world. What dad doesn't want that for his child?

We can approach God confidently, and if we ask anything that pleases Him, He hears us (1 John 5:14). I love that I can approach God confidently, knowing He has my best interests in mind. That doesn't mean I'll always get what I desire at the moment. Although God does love us so much and delights to lavish us with that love, let's admit it—what we desire to be lavished with isn't always what's best for our futures. Our Dad knows this, and He will not answer our expressed desires if we're yearning for something detrimental to our future. I desired to be lavished with a BB gun as a lad. I approached my dad with confidence, knowing that he delighted for his son to be happy. I got a Bible instead. My father in his wisdom chose to disappoint me temporarily. But his gift of the Bible led to permanent joy. It showed me the way to the life that is truly life. What an inheritance my dad gave me on that birthday!

On my birth into a new life as a son of God, my heavenly Father also gave me an amazing inheritance:

> Praise be to the God and Father of our Lord Jesus Christ! In his great mercy he has given us new birth into a living hope through the resurrection of Jesus Christ from the dead, and into an inheritance that can never perish, spoil or fade. This inheritance is kept in heaven for you. (1 Peter 1:3-4)

Remember the scene with the sheep and goats assembled before Jesus? To the sheep Jesus will say, "Come, you who are blessed by my Father; take your inheritance, the kingdom prepared for you since the creation of the world" (Matthew 25:34). Our inheritance has been in the works since the dawn of creation.

Are you in line for this amazing inheritance, this lavishing of love?

Don't miss out. Discover the life that is really life. Don't wait too long.

84

Becoming my Father

I'm sure you've all heard the saying "The apple doesn't fall far from the tree." It means you'll probably have traits and characteristics similar to those of your parents. The maxim implies that if your dad was a godly, upright, and honorable man, you stand a good chance of showing those same characteristics. If he was, well, not honorable, upright, and godly, you may have many of the same tendencies unless you make a deliberate choice to change.

My dad was godly, upright, honorable, and more. I suspect my dad's apple tree was planted on a slope, because when I dropped out of the tree, I rolled away a distance.

Dad worked hard all his life. I worked hard. Dad and I are even there. The apple moves closer to the tree.

Dad never golfed, water skied, snow skied, bowled, played tennis, or played racquet ball. I've done all of these. Sadly, I crowded them into the early years of my marriage, when the children were young. The apple rolls back down the hill.

Dad was far more diligent in prayer and Bible reading. I witnessed his Bible reading and prayer many mornings as he sat in his hickory rocker. At night, he always read from the Scriptures before sending us children off to bed. I wasn't quite that diligent with my own family. The apple rolls farther away.

Dad married a wonderful woman, my mom, and always had her by his side wherever he went. He would never consider a vacation apart from her. I took hiking trips alone many times.

The apple-and-tree adage doesn't hold true, does it? How does so much change occur in the space of one generation?

I suppose the quick and easy answer is that our lives are determined more by personal choices we make. Some of our choices are good, some are bad, some really have no significant effect on our lives and character.

I did, though, make many of my worst choices while I was married. I chased dreams, opportunity, and wealth. While fruitlessly chasing the wind, I was also running farther and farther from the apple tree. Year after year, I moved farther away from becoming my dad. I did make one good choice. I married a godly lady who attempted to kick the apple back toward the tree.

I realize I'm being critical of myself and my lifestyle early in my marriage. Someone needs to step in and give an honest evaluation of this man, your author.

No one?

Then, you see, it is up to me.

Yes, I failed. I failed many times in life. I'm not afraid to admit that. We all fail at times. We fail our children, our spouses, our friends. We fail God.

For a certainty, God is the only one who won't fail you in return.

Let's fast forward to the end of my 32-year marriage. During the final year of my wife's cancer battle, I was constantly by her side. Yes, I finished strong.

Shortly before she passed away, I overheard her speaking to a friend. Her words still ring in my mind, and I write this with tears in my eyes.

"He's my rock," she said. "He's my hero." That's high praise for an apple who had rolled such a distance from his dad's tree.

Think about these truths as they apply to your walk with Jesus. You've probably rolled quite a way from your Father's tree, too. We do fall and falter along the way. Sometimes, we may not show much family resemblance to our Father.

However, determine to finish strong. Make Jesus your rock, and make Him your hero. And His high praise and honor will reward you!

> These trials will show that your faith is genuine. It is being tested as fire tests and purifies gold... So when your faith remains strong through many trials, it will bring you much praise and glory and honor on the day when Jesus Christ is revealed to the whole world. (1 Peter 1:7 NLT)

85

Lighten Up

When I prepare for any hike, I weigh out every piece of equipment. Considering each item, I ask if it really serves a purpose and if I will use it more than once on a long hike. The items that I don't use consistently will usually lose their place in my backpack.

Because, after all, I have to carry every ounce. Weights—both necessary and unnecessary—are a burden. They slow us down.

The devil loves to weigh us down with whatever he knows will hinder our walk with God. He especially uses that one sin that always seems to trip us up. That sin might be one thing for me and another thing for you, but whatever it is, that sin needs to be chased down and captured. Your thoughts may be out of control. Those heavy weights clanging around your brain need to be captured and given to Christ. It may be that the time and choices I make watching television are keeping me from walking and talking with God. I'll need to hand the remote over to Christ. For someone else, the hurt and pain of betrayal is keeping them chained with bitterness and anger. Jesus wants to take that burden and break the chains.

Hebrews 12 tells us to lighten up. Get rid of those dead weights! We are in a race. Runners wear as little as possible in order to finish faster, and runners in the race toward Heaven also need to be free of any sin hindering them in their progress. The devil will do everything he can to hold us back and keep us from running this race well. Even if he knows we're headed home to the finish line, he's going to keep throwing things on us, hoping to interfere.

There's a great crowd watching us. They are cheering us on. Can you hear that crowd calling your name as you run? "Get rid of that weight that is hindering you!" cries a voice from the crowd. Do you recognize the weights around your ankles, on your back, or even in your head? Jesus runs beside you, offering to take them off!

Look toward the finish line!

The goal is in sight!

Our Champion, Jesus, will soon be congratulating you. "Great race! Good finish, Pilgrim. Well done."

Let Us Faith the Truth

The crowd remains and cheers as others line up to race. The crowd was there when the book of Hebrews was written, and it will remain as long as there are runners to cheer on. They won't grow tired of watching and go looking for other entertainment. They have a reason to cheer us on, a vested interest in getting us home to the finish line.

Why? Why is it so important to this group of witnesses that we lighten up, run hard, and finish strong?

The first word in Hebrews 12 is what links us back to the previous chapter and spells out what's at stake. The word is *Therefore,* and it's there for a reason.

Who are these people in the crowd? It turns out that they're folks we've read about all our lives. The writer of Hebrews calls them "the ancients." These people all had something they hoped for. Not only did they have this great hope, they were certain about it.

This certainty of hope has a name—*faith.*

Let's meet some of these spectators cheering us on. It's quite a group. It even includes some folks we might consider less than desirable.

There's Abel. God commended him as a righteous man because of the better sacrifice offered than the one brought by his brother. My buddy Enoch, the walker with God, gets a high recommendation as well. He was pleasing to God. (Won't that be a great greeting on judgment day when God says, "I am pleased with you"?) Noah gets included because he obeyed God and built an ark. Abraham graduated at the top of his class. He actually gets three mentions in this faith chapter. God invited Abraham to a place unknown; he packed up and obeyed God, living the rest of his life as a stranger in a foreign country. He lived in tents, but his hope looked forward to a city God was building that had foundations. He even called God the architect. Abe's second commendation was for believing God when he was told he would become a dad in his old age, and the third mention is his obedience when God tested him, telling him to offer his son Isaac as a sacrifice. I'm sure Abraham recalled God's promise that Isaac would continue the family line. That would be impossible if Isaac died. Did Abraham believe that if he obeyed and did sacrifice his son, God would bring Isaac back from the dead? I don't know. I do know Abraham prepared to do what God told him to do.

Perhaps this high standing with God for all his trust, obedience, and faith is why we see Abraham standing side by side with Lazarus the beggar in Luke 16. Somewhere in the lower regions of the earth is a place where the ancients went when they passed on. This would include anyone who believed in and had this great hope about God's future city with foundations. Another area—within shouting distance, it seems—is the place where those who rejected God awaited judgment. A barrier separates these two places.

In Jesus' story in Luke 16, one day a rich man on the hopeless side of this great divide looked across to the hope side and saw Abraham and a fellow who looked familiar. Lazarus was a mess in life. His body covered with sores, he laid at the gate of this rich man's house, begging for crumbs that dropped from the rich man's table.

Apparently, Lazarus and Abraham had become friends. Abraham knew Lazarus's story. The rich man now becomes the beggar, imploring them for one drop of water. But Lazarus would not be going across that great divide. The rich man had his chance, and waited too long.

Oh yes, there are others of hope. Isaac, Jacob, Joseph, and of course, Moses. Moses made a choice many of us might have hesitated to make. He was raised in luxury but made a deliberate choice to be mistreated alongside his family of origin. For him, the treasures of Egypt were of lesser value than the reward awaiting him after his death. A prostitute also made the faith list. That should give all sinners hope that redemption is possible and available.

What does all this have to do with us runners, running our own faith race?

This crowd needs us!

Isn't that amazing?

They were all given hope about a future home with foundations. A promise was given to them. They believed this promise and longed for its completion. One thing holds up the culmination of this promise: Us!

Yes, us.

The people of faith all await perfection, God's perfection. They are waiting for the fulfillment of God's promise of this perfect city with foundations built for perfect people.

Here's the rub: Only with us runners here on earth will they be made perfect. Imagine that. They need us. That makes me feel kind of important. We are part of God's plan for perfection.

Run hard! Run fast! Throw off everything, especially that one sin that still weighs you down. Get rid of it. Strain for the finish line. "Become perfect with us!" the crowd shouts.

87

The First Supper

I hate endings. I've had too many difficult endings; I'm weary of grieving endings. I grieved the loss of my wife of 32 years. That led me to give up a good job to take a hike of healing. But I grieved the job I had enjoyed. The hike led to new love, the highest of highs. That new love ended so abruptly—the lowest of lows. I've grieved that loss throughout the writing of this book.

Now I'm brought to another ending. This book draws to a close.

This volume has been vastly different than any of my previous writings. I've invited you along with me as I grappled with the loss of love and trust. This has been an account of my journey with two loves. One ended, and another began a new season of growth.

I've renewed my vow to follow Jesus. He is the one person who won't let us down.

That's always the way it is: An ending leads to new beginnings. But besides hating endings, I also embrace new beginnings reluctantly. So you can understand how the transitions of life have taken a toll on me.

Endings are inevitable in this life. In my journey, another ending looms on the horizon. This one is the most important ending of all. I now have more years in my rear-view mirror than in front of my windshield. I hope to be around for some time yet, but I've also made other plans.

You see, I've received an invitation to a wedding. (Not my own, although I hope that does become a reality yet in my earthly journey.) I've been invited to a wedding taking place in the evening, date uncertain. Yes, a supper wedding.

I have part in the wedding. I suppose that makes me special. Me, special? Yes, although that thought stretches my mind to the edges. Because I really didn't deserve even an invitation. I'm not that good a person. I've said things I shouldn't have. I've done things I shouldn't have. I've been lied to and lied about. I've been deceived by folks who said they cared. And I've been deceptive myself at times. I've been both underestimated and overestimated. I've had bad words spoken about me and also many good words spoken. I often wonder if I actually make a difference in anyone else's life. I've doubted God and I've trusted God. I always give folks the benefit of the doubt; I default to trusting people, and I've been rewarded for that and let down by that. I've had trust broken by loved ones, and I've broken trust.

Yes, I'm describing myself and my life, and I believe this also describes many of my readers. It certainly describes my friend David. But he and I are men after God's own heart. We have accepted the fact that God loves us and wants a relationship with us. That's why I've received that wedding-supper invitation.

Supper comes at the ending of a day. When Dad came out on the front porch and called all his chillens to the supper table, we all gathered round that table and prayed together, ate together, and spoke about the events of the day. As bedtime approached, we gathered in the living room, and Dad read from the Bible. Then off to bed we went.

Then the concert started. One of the songs Mom and Dad sang together was "Come home, it's supper time."

> When I was just a boy in days of childhood,
> I used to play till evening shadows come.
> Then winding down an old familiar pathway,
> I heard my mother call at set of sun:
>
> Come home, come home,
> It's supper time,
> The shadows lengthen fast.
> Come home, come home,
> It's supper time,
> We're going home at last.
>
> In visions now I see her standing yonder,
> And her familiar voice I hear once more.
> The banquet table's ready up in heaven,
> It's supper time upon the golden shore.
>   (Ira F. Stanphill, 1950)

My mom and dad were married 68 years and together made a home for me and my sisters that gave us a taste of Heaven. I often wonder how God chooses who is born into which home. Why was I so fortunate to have this home? I lived in that environment for 23 years.

When Dad was 90 years old, his mind started to fade a bit. He often asked my mother to take him for a drive. "I want to go home," he often said. He gave Mom directions as she drove; he was seeking a place he called home. I think he was trying to find his own mom and dad. How he longed to hear his mother call again, "Come home, it's supper time!" She and Grandfather were already both in Heaven, and Dad needed to await his own invitation.

I often reflect on our supper time conversations around the kitchen table. I can still see Dad or Mom coming out onto the front porch to call us all to supper. How I long to hear that once again.

However, there's an even greater calling to supper awaiting me. It's only fitting to end this book by going to the ending of another book, the Bible, where we read, "Blessed are those who are invited to the wedding supper of the Lamb" (Revelation 19:9).

I can see it now, and I've heard the invitation. "Come home, Paul. It's supper time!"

In my imagination, I'll approach those glistening walls of Heaven. I'll wave that invitation wildly. Yes, I have RSVP'd.

Jesus himself will appear. "Welcome home. We've been expecting you. Come in, you're just in time for supper. Your place at the table awaits. There are people at the table here because of you. They want to see you."

"You mean I made a difference? How's that possible?"

"You made a good choice. You walked with God."

And as I sit down to celebrate, I want the last line of my obituary to read, "He didn't wait too long."

Going Even Deeper

This book has been deeply personal. I'm hoping that what I've shared so openly with you has touched you in deeply personal ways as well.

Here are questions to help you plow deeper and plant more seeds for new life. I'm guessing that if you are honest, these questions will be revealing and quite possibly uncomfortable. You might want to use these for your own private introspection or for discussion in a group you trust.

This introspection will be most effective if you ask the Spirit to lead you to truth and also jot down Scriptures that help you, or, as I did, snap a photo and save them on your cell phone.

Chapters 1 – 23: Valleys, Wilderness, and Storms

1. What goals, plans, hopes, and desires are you postponing, waiting for a time that you may never have? What sandcastles have you already seen washed away?

2. Can you look back at your life and see the valleys, wildernesses, or storms you have walked through? God allowed that storm in your life. He had a purpose. Can you now see God's presence and working during that time?

3. Perhaps you're in a wilderness of pain right now. Can you say, with David, "God, I trust in you"? If you find that difficult to say right now, what might help you find the faith to trust Him in this time?

4. Jesus says, "Come to me, and I'll give you rest." What rest do you want from Jesus? Is there a burden you're tired of carrying and want to give to Him?

5. Do you ever hear Jesus telling you to get out of your boat? Remember, He told Peter to "Come" in the middle of a storm. Has He asked you to have courage and "Come"? Is He asking that of you right now?

Chapters 24 – 41: Heart Conditions

1. Here we find thoughts on deception, unforgiveness, and rejection. Is your heart struggling with any of these?

2. What did you understand this line to mean: *Pass the manna, please.* (Page 95) How might this apply to your life?

3. Review Chapter 32. Take each of the heart conditions explained in Jesus' parable and explain how each would look played out in daily life. Which best describes your heart?

4. Review Chapter 33. Give specific examples of how we are double-minded and double-hearted. What is the cure for this?

5. Review Chapter 34. Has your heart been plowed? What new life has then sprouted?

6. Review Chapter 35. What in "The Stained-Glass Heart" spoke to you?

7. Review Chapter 36. Did anything in "You Are Loved" touch your heart?

8. Is there anything in your heart that you want God to transform into a new creature?

Chapters 42 – 59: Traveling Toward Your Expiration Date

1. If you actually knew the day you are set to expire, what would you do differently today?

2. To many, the Holy Spirit is only a vague idea, "a mysterious presence we can't really relate to or know." Can you explain what you know of the Spirit? Who is He to you? Through these chapters, has the Spirit revealed to you anything new about Himself?

3. Are you contemplating life changes? Are you postponing because you don't have the courage to make a hard choice? What is holding you back? What can give you the necessary courage?

4. How has God spoken to you in the last week? Has He given you obvious signs? Or can you look back at a difficult

time in your life and see signposts He gave you but you missed (or ignored)?

5. If you died tonight, what do you suppose your obituary would say? What would you like it to say? Is there any specific wording or phrases you definitely want included? (If so, let your family or friends know about this.)

6. *In your life, you can write the book you always planned to write, or you can write a book you can't imagine. You can take a journey you have planned out in detail—which leaves little room for a close walk with God—or you can take courage and have faith and follow your Guide. He's looking for hearts that are courageous enough to follow Him.*
Does this quote light a fire of longing in your heart? Spend some time looking through Scripture and jot down specific verses that bolster your courage and faith to follow Jesus wherever He leads you.

Chapters 60 – 87: Becoming Enoch

1. Read Ephesians 4:24 and Colossians 3:10; 1 Corinthians 10:31 and Isaiah 43:7; Colossians 3:2 and Matthew 6:20. What are the most important goals we need to keep in sight?

2. What distracts you from these goals? What will correct your course and vision?

3. Has the Spirit been speaking to you about any weight that is bogging you down in the race toward the finish line?

4. Are you carrying a burden of unforgiveness? Or do you need forgiveness for something you've done? Are you ready to hand that over to Jesus?

5. *"Our inheritance has been in the works since the dawn of creation."* What does it mean to you to be "joint heirs with Christ"?

Author's Note

There are several subjects in which I am well versed. One is travel stories. You've followed many of my travels, and I truly do appreciate that you've hiked and biked and paddled with me.

Thank *you* for buying this book and sharing this journey with me. As you have seen, this book is very different. I have been in a very different state of mind and heart as I wrote. As I've said in these pages, I honestly don't know why God has chosen to give me the gift of authorship, but I continue to be amazed and grateful for it.

A follow-up on this healing journey will be coming in my next volume, *The Miracle Journey*.

Again, I want to thank my editor, Elaine Starner, for working with me on every project since *Hiking Through*. She deserves an extra thank-you for meeting the urgent deadline on this book. (Or so she says...)

Whatever it is the Spirit has been talking to you about as you've read these pages, *don't wait too long* to follow His lead!

Paul Stutzman

GET TO KNOW PAUL STUTZMAN at

www.paulstutzman.com
www.hikingthrough.com
www.facebook.com/pvstutzman
pstutzman@roadrunner.com

OTHER BOOKS BY PAUL STUTZMAN

The Wandering Home Series (Fiction)
Book One: The Wanderers
Book Two: Wandering Home
Book Three: Wander No More

Adventure Memoir
Hiking Through
One Man's Journey to Peace and Freedom on the Appalachian Trail

Biking Across America
My Coast-to-Coast Adventure and the People I Met Along the Way

Mississippi Misadventure

Pilgrims: On the Camino de Santiago

Hiking Israel (Formerly titled *The 13th Disciple*)
From Galilee to Jerusalem

With Author Serena Miller
More Than Happy: The Wisdom of Amish Parenting

Children's Picture Books
The Cloud Factory
The Great Cloud Rescue (coming in 2022)

www.ingramcontent.com/pod-product-compliance
Lightning Source LLC
Chambersburg PA
CBHW032101090426
42743CB00007B/195